D1073375

FIRST GARDEN

How to Get Started in
Southwest Gardening

∎

Janice Busco
with Rob Proctor

Photography by Charles Mann
and Rob Proctor

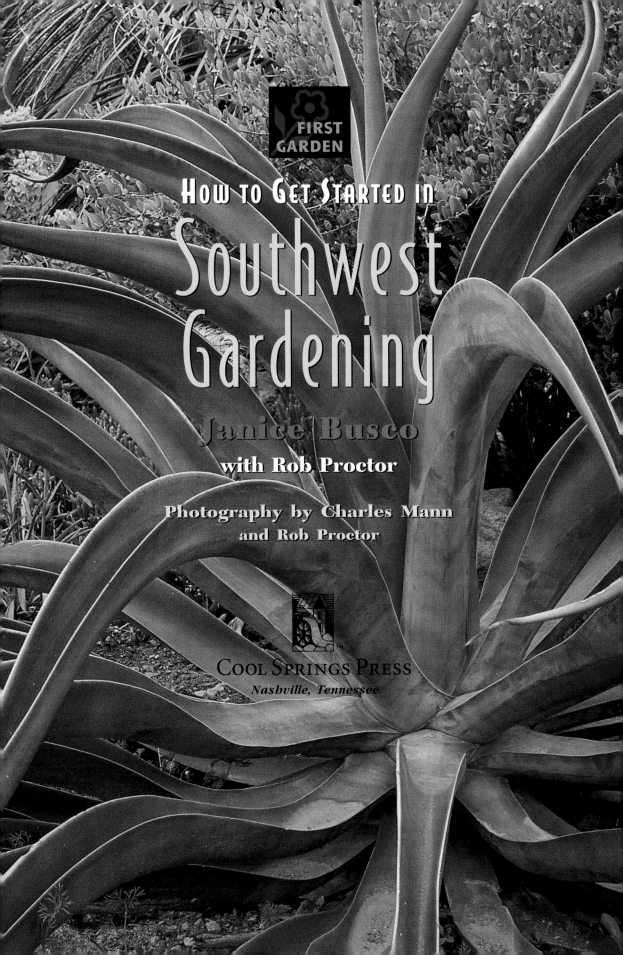

FIRST GARDEN

How to Get Started in
Southwest
Gardening

Janice Busco

with Rob Proctor

Photography by Charles Mann
and Rob Proctor

COOL SPRINGS PRESS
Nashville, Tennessee

Introduction text copyright © 2005 Rob Proctor
Text copyright © 2005 Janice Busco
Photography copyright © 2005 Charles Mann, except where otherwise noted
(see photography credits on page 10).

All rights reserved. No part of this book may be reproduced or transmitted in any form, or by any means, electronic or mechanical, including photocopying, recording, or by any information storage and retrieval system, without permission in writing from the publisher.

Published by Cool Springs Press,
a Division of Thomas Nelson, Inc.,
P. O. Box 141000, Nashville, Tennessee 37214.

Library of Congress Cataloging-in-Publication Data
Busco, Janice.
   How to get started in southwest gardening / Janice Busco, with Rob Proctor.
      p. cm. — (First garden)
   Includes index.
   ISBN 1-59186-160-8
   1. Gardening—Southwestern States. 2. Plants, Ornamenta—Southwestern States.
I. Proctor, Rob. II. Title. III. Series.
   SB453.2.S68B87 2005
   635.9'0979--dc22

                                                    2004030932

Printed in the United States of America
10 9 8 7 6 5 4 3 2 1

Book Development & Project Management: Marlene Blessing, Marlene Blessing Editorial
Copyediting: Melanie Stafford
Design & Formatting: Constance Bollen, cb graphics
First Garden Series Consultant: Darrell Trout
Map: Bill Kersey, Kersey Graphics

FRONT COVER: Images clockwise from upper left are moonflower, Indian blanket, agave, and golden barrel cactus. Photographs copyright © Charles Mann.

BACK COVER: Butterfly milkweed. Photograph copyright © Charles Mann.

Cool Springs Press books may be purchased in bulk
for educational, business, fundraising, or sales promotional use.
For information, please email SpecialMarkets@ThomasNelson.com.

Visit the Thomas Nelson Web site at www.ThomasNelson.com
and the Cool Springs Press Web site at www.coolspringspress.net.

To my parents,

who raised me up in a garden with hummingbirds,

freesias, adobe clay, and sweet limes.

And to our neighbors,

who freely shared their sweet peas,

giant sunflowers, figs, parrots,

and wild cotton.

Red bird-of-paradise (*Caesalpinia pulcherrima*)

ACKNOWLEDGMENTS

Thanks to Wade Albrecht, Joanne Baggs, Glenda M. Raikes-Bennett, Hattie Braun, Cheryl Casey, Tim Crews, Cado Daily, Carol Daily, Patrick Grant, Mar-Elise Hill, Jonathan Holden and Ina Miloff, Chuck McDougal, Mary McCormick, Robert Pape, Patrick Pynes, Jean Searle, Loni Shapiro, Deb Sparrow, Lael Tennyson, and Julie Woodman for sharing their knowledge and experience.

I compiled the table "Which Native Plants Are Right for You? Typical Native Plants for Southwestern Gardens" (page 71) from information found in *Biotic Communities: Southwestern United States and Northwestern Mexico*, edited by David E. Brown, University of Utah Press. I highly recommend this work for readers who want to delve more deeply into the natural origins and ecology of their southwestern native garden plants.

My gratitude, also, to Lance, Noor, Cosmo, EZ, Hunter, Mango, Bob I and Bob II Diskan for taking care of my heart and home, and for making me laugh.

And finally, thanks to Marlene Blessing for creating and sustaining First Gardens, and to Constance Bollen for her enticing and accessible book design.

FIRST GARDEN

SECTION 1 / 15

Your First Garden by Rob Proctor

SOUTHWEST GARDENING

SECTION 2 / 65

Your Southwest Garden
by Janice Busco

PHOTOGRAPHY CREDITS

All photography is by Charles Mann *(photo spread page 2–3, taken at Boyce Thompson Arboretum, Superior, AZ.)*, except the following:

Rob Proctor: 17, 18, 21, 24, 25, 27, 29, 30, 31, 33 upper left and 33 upper right, 34, 35, 37, 38, 40, 42, 44, 45, 48, 49, 51, 57, 59, 63, 86, 98

Liz Ball: 156 top

For First-Time Gardeners Everywhere

No matter what part of the country you live in, it is possible to create a vibrant garden that adds beauty to your home and to your *life*. The First Garden series of books are meant for anyone who is just beginning to create his or her first garden. To someone who is new to gardening, a successful, thriving garden may seem like a feat to which only professionals and those with green thumbs can aspire. However, with a clear introduction to the basics—understanding your region (climate, soil, and topography); knowing the plants that grow best in your region; applying good design principles; and learning how to maintain and boost your garden's performance—you will quickly be able to start a garden. And do so with confidence! Before you know it, you may be sharing your garden dos and don'ts with your neighbor across the way.

In Section One of the book, you'll find easy-to-understand guidance to help you master the basics. As you read through this general introduction to gardening, written by nationally recognized garden expert Rob Proctor, you'll see photographs that aren't necessarily specific to your region. These are used to illustrate a design principle, technique, planting combination, or other important concept. Don't worry that your region has been forgotten! The entire final portion of the book, Section Two, is exclusively devoted to gardening specifics for your home turf. In addition to learning such things as how to improve your soil, when to plant bulbs, how to prune a tree or bush, and what kind of troubleshooting you may need to do, you'll also get a complete list of 50 sure-fire plants for your garden. Our regional garden experts have carefully selected these plants to enable you to have the best start possible as you begin what we hope will become a lifetime activity for you.

Like most pursuits, gardening takes time and patience to master. The First Garden books are designed to give you a reliable, can't-miss start. In addition to learning how to grow plants in your region, you will discover the process of turning your landscape into a beautiful, nurturing extension of your home. Even if you are beginning with only a few containers of plants on your deck or patio, you'll soon find that gardening rewards you with colors and scents that make your environment infinitely more satisfying.

With this book as your portable "garden expert," you can begin a great new adventure, knowing that you have friendly, clear advice that will keep you on the garden path. Most of all, we want to welcome you to gardening!

The Editors at Cool Springs Press

USDA Cold Hardiness Zone Map

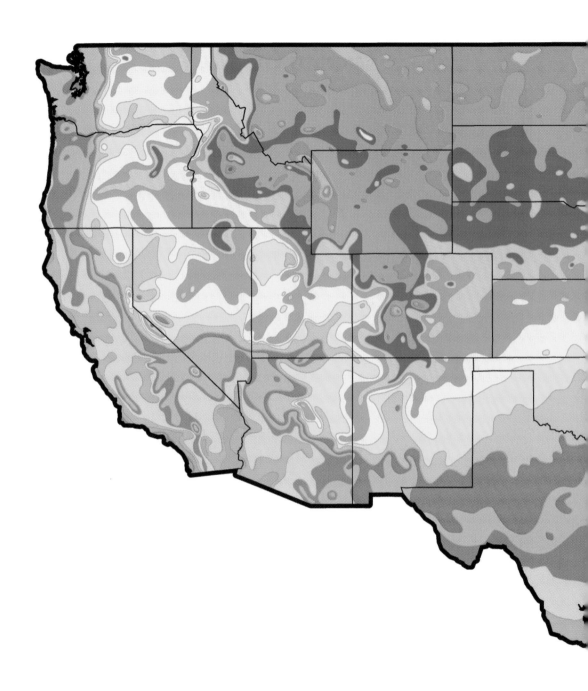

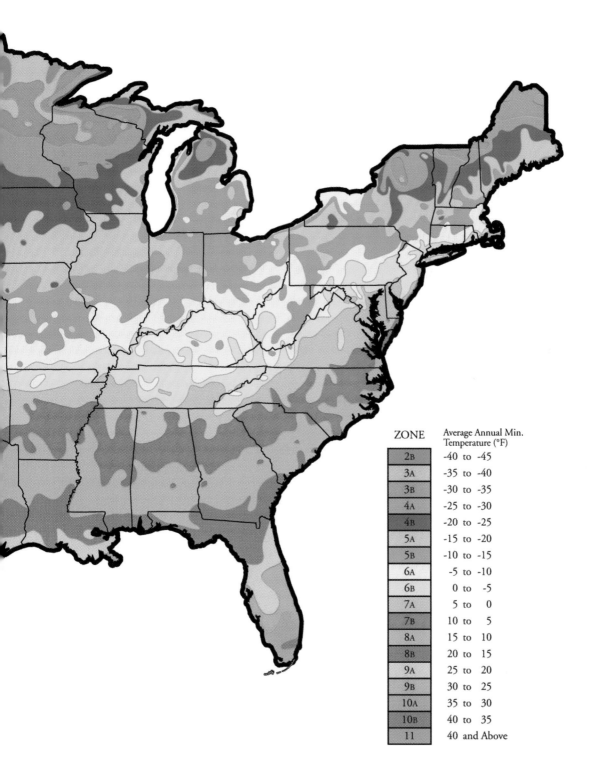

ZONE	Average Annual Min. Temperature (°F)	
2B	-40	to	-45
3A	-35	to	-40
3B	-30	to	-35
4A	-25	to	-30
4B	-20	to	-25
5A	-15	to	-20
5B	-10	to	-15
6A	-5	to	-10
6B	0	to	-5
7A	5	to	0
7B	10	to	5
8A	15	to	10
8B	20	to	15
9A	25	to	20
9B	30	to	25
10A	35	to	30
10B	40	to	35
11	40 and Above		

Section 1

Your First Garden

Your first garden is unique. It might start as a blank canvas at a newly built house, without so much as a blade of grass. Or it could be an established landscape that you wish to make your own. Your approach will depend on your scenario. Your first garden might not even include land at the moment; perhaps, if you're an urban dweller, you've decided to garden on a rooftop or balcony.

Making a new garden is complex, intimidating, engrossing, and thrilling. It's all about color, design, and placement. Our visions dance before our eyes like sugar plum fairies. We're capable once again of that magic we used to know as children. My friend Wendy just started her first garden, and I helped her with some planning and took her shopping for plants. We filled her SUV and she rushed home to plant. She called me to say she was "enthralled in the madness" and some of our initial planning went out the window as her creative juices flowed. Good for her!

It would be rare if a garden turned out exactly as planned. However, countless TV makeover shows lead us to believe that this can happen. We see the plan, then some fast-motion digging and planting, then the finished project and the dazed surprise of the happy homeowner. This

---

Visions spring to life in the form of satiny Iceland poppies, coral bells, and tiny 'Zing Rose' dianthus

Lush and romantic, this garden features roses scrambling onto a wagon wheel, coral Jupiter's beard, spikes of fireweed, and a pink skirt of Mexican evening primrose.

all happens in the course of several days, boiled down to less than a 30-minute show. But then what? What happens to the new garden afterward?

Don't get me wrong. I like these shows and often get good design ideas from them. But without a follow-up, we don't have any idea what became of the transformation we've just witnessed. Did the owner water enough? Too much? Did the plants get enough sun? Did those vines cover the new trellis that hides that ugly garage wall? Did the perennials fill in like a soft carpet around the new pond? Or did bindweed and thistle sprout everywhere, choke out the new plants, and return the area to its former dilapidated, dismal state?

My own first garden was poorly planned, badly designed, chock-full of mistakes—and absolutely wonderful. Filled with boundless enthusiasm and unwarranted confidence from growing up in a gardening family, I blundered my way within a few years to creating a garden that was the subject of glamorous layouts in three magazines. In the process, I devoured hundreds of gardening books, subscribed to every horticultural magazine and newsletter I could find, visited every public and private garden I could, and lost twenty pounds.

I planted, transplanted, divided, amended, pruned, mulched, whacked, hacked, hoed, pinched, seeded, and fertilized until my thumb turned green. Making your first garden can be one of the most stimulating and creative experiences of your life. It might also be frustrating, confusing, and occasionally heartbreaking. It all depends on how you do it. You can take small steps or giant leaps. I'm a leaper myself, but I appreciate the cautious, practical approach, of which I'm incapable. The kind of people who plan meticulously might need a big sketch pad and several notebooks (you're probably mentally planning a shopping trip for this purpose at exactly 4:45 P.M. tomorrow afternoon). And it wouldn't hurt to construct a storyboard (borrow the bulletin board from your kid's room) of pictures and articles clipped from magazines, photos from friends' and public gardens, and even key words you want to remember as overriding themes. "Romantic," "lush," "bountiful," and "low-maintenance" don't go in the same sentence, by the way. But we'll talk about realistic maintenance later.

> My own first garden was poorly planned, badly designed, chock-full of mistakes— and absolutely wonderful.

Your notebooks can start to fill with color swatches; plant "wish lists"; clippings from the paper; brochures from fence, irrigation, and patio furniture companies; and preliminary budget figures. This might sound a bit like decorating a living room (and indeed your garden will be a "living" room), but there's a difference. With an indoor space you actually reach a point where it's considered finished. With a garden—as an evolving place—it's never completely finished, just done "for now." A garden that doesn't change is not only impossible, but I guarantee you would find it boring.

■ Discovering Your Inner Gardener

When you begin to garden, there are so many considerations it's tough to know where to start. So let's start with you. Do you like gardening work? That means watering, fertilizing, digging, planting, pruning, and all that? Not to mention the dreaded "W" word—weeding. Unlike tennis or ballet, gardening doesn't require any particular talents or physical attributes such as grace or brute strength. It just takes industriousness. People who like to keep house or fix cars, for example, may make fine gardeners, because the plans of attack to get the job done are similar.

Gardening is the number-one pastime in our country. Perhaps not everyone practices it to a refined degree, but this does mean that, in general, we enjoy the pleasures of working in the soil and raising flowers and vegetables. Your garden is what you make it. You'll be surprised how quickly you'll pick up the knowledge and skills to make yours beautiful and productive. Gardening is part art and part science, so there's room for everybody—right- or left-brainers— to get into the act. A friend of mine once called gardening the "slowest of the performing arts." You're the director and the plants you grow are the stars and supporting players.

As the director of your horticultural extravaganza (as well as the set designer, head writer, and entire technical crew), start with your vision. Some people might begin with a low-budget home movie, and others envision an epic blockbuster. Our inspirations come from many sources— childhood memories, books and magazines, and travels. And since I've drawn an analogy to the movies, let's acknowledge that many of us find inspiration on the silver screen as well. Sometimes

I feel my garden resembles the one in *The Secret Garden*. Before the children cleaned it up. (By the way, those were remarkably skilled kids, outperforming a crew of at least 20 landscapers.)

■ Blueprints for the Garden

As you plan your garden and its "rooms," take a look at what you've got—at ground level and below. City and suburban dwellers often live in a house that sits on a square, flat lot. Even a rooftop or balcony gardener usually deals with a level rectangular space. On the other hand, perhaps you live amidst hills, valleys, embankments, or even streams or ponds on your property. Your nearest neighbor may be feet or miles away.

It's probably time to clarify the difference between a landscape and a garden. Although the two are connected, there are some differences. A landscape applies to everything on the property, but most specifically trees, shrubs, and hardscape (walkways, walls, driveways, decks, patios). A landscape may include "garden areas" as a part of its overall scheme. The traditional American landscape typically features a lot of lawn, "foundation plantings" of shrubs that hug the house, and various trees placed for shade. It's a nice, familiar picture, perhaps with a strip of geraniums or petunias bordering the walk. Or maybe there's a flowerbed skirting the row of junipers or yews lined up under the eaves of the house.

The footprint of your house, any outbuildings, and adjacent buildings define your site. One way or the other, you may wish to make a blueprint of your property to draw and dream upon. It doesn't need to be exactly to scale (or even blue). I wouldn't even recommend doing much detailed planning on it since one-dimensional blueprints rarely translate into beautiful three-dimensional gardens. Just use it to familiarize yourself with all the features of your existing site (or lack of them) and for the placement of present and future walkways, driveways, patios, walls, trees, and specific garden areas or features. These could be things such as herb, cutting, or vegetable gardens as well as borders, ponds, play areas, and so forth. I often sketch on a legal pad to help me plan or revamp an area. (I once designed a friend's garden on a cocktail napkin, but that's another story that taught me I need a bigger piece of paper.)

If you picture creating a garden that is more unique, you won't need to exclude any of these traditional elements. Instead, you'll treat them somewhat differently and focus more directly on flowers and vegetables and their relationships to everything else on the property. In this scenario, there's a nearly constant, hands-on relationship between you and the plants, far beyond a weekly mowing or annual hedge trimming. If you really like plants, you can transform any static landscape into an active garden.

■ About Soil

What color is your thumb? People who meet me often feel obliged to apologize for their black thumbs. "I kill everything," they tell me. There's no such thing as a black thumb. Everybody can garden. Plants—like pets—need water, food, a suitable place to live, and occasional grooming. Green thumbs aren't born, they're made. The origin of the term stems from the fact that gardeners put excessive wear and tear on their thumbs and forefingers. As they pinch petunias or pull pigweed, the green sap stains eventually become engrained for most of the gardening season. My thumb's not a classic green but more of a dirty olive tone. Let's not mention my knuckles and nails, which are accented by various cuts, scrapes, and punctures.

You don't need to ruin your hands. Sensible glove-wearing gardeners still deserve the title green thumb. You can earn it, too. Learn the basics and build on those, just the way you'd approach any new pastime such as cooking, tennis, sewing, or carpentry.

Okay, former black thumbs: get started. Dig a spadeful of soil. (If you're a rooftop or balcony gardener, skip this and go buy some potting soil.) Squeeze a handful. Does it stick together into a mud ball? You have clay. That's most of us. If the ball of soil falls apart, you've got sand. It's an easier soil to dig, but dries out more quickly. If you're extremely lucky, you're blessed with rich, black "Iowa cornfield" soil that gardeners crave (in which case you're probably reading this in Iowa). Don't worry. Both clay and sandy soil can be amended to grow some traditional plants. On the other hand, a good many plants are so adaptable that they'll grow well in almost any kind of soil.

Once you've done some experimenting, you can decide what—if anything—you want to do to your soil. I actually don't amend soil, but grow what wants to grow in that soil. I've often read or seen experts who recommend a soil test. I've never done one. I wouldn't have a clue what it meant if I had 100 parts magnesium

Green thumbs aren't born, they're made.

A garden planted in unimproved clay soil, rarely irrigated, supports many drought-tolerant perennials including varieties of penstemons and bright Jupiter's beard.

per million. Unless you suspect that your soil has an actual problem (such as being missing after the builders finished the house) or has some sort of contamination, I can't imagine the value of a test unless you want to grow rare alpine plants from Switzerland. Even if your soil has been pounded and pulverized by heavy equipment, you don't need a soil test to tell you it's been compacted and that with just a little more pressure will turn into diamonds. Most people have the kind of soil that everybody else in their neighborhood has. What's growing there? Does it look healthy? If the trees are dying and lawns are sickly, don't get a soil test—call the Environmental Protection Agency.

Your soil will actually teach you as you go along what it's capable of doing. It may not support absolutely every type of plant you might want to grow (I'll never have blueberries), but odds are it has plenty of potential. For extreme sand or clay, you may decide to amend or alter your soil or bring in topsoil for plants with specific needs (I would need to create an acidic bog to grow blueberries). But first explore what your soil can do before you begin a wholesale radical makeover that will forever alter its composition.

Don't just start adding ingredients willy-nilly. Many books often recommend adding lime to the soil as a matter of course. The assumption is that most plants do best if grown in a soil that is about neutral on the pH scale. This advice may be all well and good in Cleveland or Boston where the soil pH is on the acid side, for the lime would reduce the acidity. But for gardeners in the West, which generally has an alkaline soil, the lime would be a waste of time, like giving "The Rock" a gym membership for his birthday. The point is to be familiar with your soil type and composition, but don't stress about it.

■ Weather and Gardening Zones

Before you start thinking about planting, determine in which climate zone you live. The U.S. Department of Agriculture (USDA) issues a detailed map, found at the front of this book, that illustrates these zones throughout the country. Based primarily on average minimum temperatures, the map helps you determine which plants will survive in your area. Almost all the plants you buy will be rated as to the zones where they are hardy, meaning where they'll survive an average winter. Most nurseries in your region only carry plants that are appropriate to it. But if you purchase plants online or by mail, you should be aware of your zone so you don't end up planting a tropical palm in Minnesota.

Many gardeners expand their options by clever gardening known as "zone denial."

IN THE ZONE

The USDA climate zone map is a good aid in helping you decide what to grow, but it has its limitations. For example, it doesn't take into account rainfall, humidity, and, most importantly, high temperatures. These factors also affect plant survival. You'll find that Chicago, Denver, and Hartford are all categorized as zone 5, but their actual growing conditions vary considerably. Rainfall, humidity, and summer heat—as well as soil type—may play as great a role in plant performance as winter low temperatures. Southern gardeners sometimes find that plants considered hardy for their zone won't thrive in their summer heat or need a colder winter dormancy than southern climes provide. Tulips are a case in point. It all sounds terribly complicated, but as you visit local nurseries and gardens, you'll get the hang of it. You'll soon start to get a grasp of what wants to grow in your area.

MICROCLIMATES

Adhering to the zone designations may help you play it safe, but many gardeners expand their options by clever gardening known as "zone denial." After all, plants can't read. If they receive the conditions that allow them to thrive, they will. This is where knowing your garden site intimately is vital. Throughout it there are "microclimates," little pockets formed by topography, fences, trees, and walls. Your house offers the most differentiations. Southern and western exposures are usually hotter and sunnier; northern and eastern exposures, cooler and shadier. The placement of trees can moderate or enhance these conditions.

A hill or outcropping may afford at least two distinct microclimates in much the same way as your house does. Lower areas tend to be cooler and, because cold air sinks, often freeze earlier than higher ground, as well as collecting and holding moisture. Knowing this helps you to position plants that prefer either well-drained soil (on a slope) or moist soil (in a hog wallow). Both air and water drain in the same manner on a large scale. Cold air often "flows" along streams and rivers, making low-lying areas "frost pockets" and higher ground "banana belts." If you're in a low-lying area, there's not much you can do about this, of course, except to be more cautious about setting out tender plants in spring or protecting them in the fall. If you're on a hilltop, you can just feel smug. But hilltops may get fierce winds (in gardening, there's a plus and minus to every condition). Knowing the direction of the prevailing wind helps prevent mistakes as well; otherwise you may be staking your delphiniums with rebar.

Paving and foundations, as well as rocks and rock outcrops also affect plant performance, either for better or worse, depending on the plant. Some plants revel in the extra heat from driveways, walkways, and foundations, and others can't stand baking. Many plants also like to get their roots beneath rocks and paving not only because of the extra heat, but because the mass of the stone moderates the surrounding temperatures by virtue of its slow heating and cooling. Rock gardeners exploit these possibilities to the max, with every nook and cranny offering a potential microclimate for a special plant.

Wherever you live, you can create a beautiful garden. Gardeners often envy others who live in different climates, usually because of particular plants that grow beautifully in that environment. By all means, experiment to see if you can achieve similar results. But don't get hung up on a certain flower that has little intention of performing for you. Yes, I've made attempts to grow azaleas and rhododendrons that I admire in friends' gardens in Virginia. And failed. So I'm content to visit them in spring and enjoy their good fortune. They come to see me, too, to admire western specialties that their gardens can't accommodate successfully, like prickly poppies and penstemons.

Although we often equate an abundance of moisture with successful gardening, it's only because the spectacular gardens in rainy regions get most of the good press. Lovely, original gardens are found within every region of our country. They are filled with the plants that want to grow there. Some may be native wildflowers, and others may originate in areas around the

A rock-terraced slope provides good drainage and extra heat for purple verbena, agave, and ice plants, with a backdrop of golden black-eyed Susans.

world with similar climate and soil. Fortunately for all of us, there's an enormous pool of plants that offer amazing abilities to adapt to a wide spectrum of conditions. Like our country itself, your new garden is likely to become a melting pot of flowers and styles from many lands—with your very own personal stamp.

■ Plant Names: Why Latin?

There's no escaping it. You need a little Latin—not much, but a little. Every living thing, animal and plant, is classified scientifically using a system that speaks Latin. To keep the millions of distinct forms of life in some sort of reasonable order, they all have a scientific name, much like our first and last names. It avoids duplication. If you looked in the phone book under Mary Jones or Bob Smith, you understand how confusing it could get if we just called plants "bluebell" or "daisy."

Most people know more scientific plant names than they think. Even non-gardeners are familiar with *chrysanthemum, geranium, lobelia, dahlia, crocus, phlox, gardenia, verbena, begonia,* and *petunia*. Others aren't much of a stretch, such as *rosa* for rose, *lilium* for lily, *tulipa* for tulip, or *hyacinthus* for hyacinth.

Within any genus of plants or animals there are individual species. Let's start with people. We all belong to the genus *Homo*, meaning human. And our species is *sapiens*, meaning wise or intelligent. We belong to the classification "intelligent human." We don't need to draw this distinction very often since the rest of the members of our genus are extinct. *Homo erectus* was "standing man," who apparently could walk upright but wasn't known for his brain. The traits of particular plants are often noted in their species name, called the specific epitaph, such as their color, habit, size, leaf shape, their resemblance to something else, what habitat they grow in, their country or region of origin, or something like that. They don't always make a whole lot of sense. Sometimes they honor a botanist who first discovered them or somebody to whom the discoverer wanted to suck up. After all, who wouldn't want a plant named for them? Most plants were named hundreds of years ago, although new discoveries occasionally crop up in rain forests.

When plant breeders get involved, plants acquire yet another name. Say that you, as a plant breeder, cross two different species to create a brand-new offspring with distinctly different characteristics from the two parents. Or say that, as a sharp-eyed gardener or nursery owner, you spot an unusual variation in an otherwise uniform batch of plants. What do you do? Name it, of course, for your wife, husband, mother, daughter, or a celebrity you admire. Or if you're more creative, you go for something more lyrical or amusing. That's why we have *Anemone* x *hybrida* 'Honorine Jobert' (named for the guy's daughter), the hybrid tea rose 'Dolly Parton' (a voluptuous flower), and the self-descriptive petunia 'Purple Wave' (the color really flows). I've always hoped to create a new color of the trailing annual *Bacopa* and call it 'Cabana'. The gardening world is waiting. . . .

Penstemon fanciers need to know the scientific names of pink *Penstemon palmeri* and purple *P. strictus*.

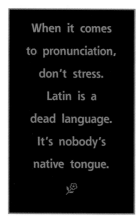

When it comes to pronunciation, don't stress. Latin is a dead language. It's nobody's native tongue.

As for the scientific names, we don't use them very much except for perennials. Not too many people say *quercus* instead of oak or *curcubita* instead of squash (unless they're really, really snobbish). Whenever a common name will do, use it. Most gardeners—in my opinion—should just talk about daylilies, Russian sage, and yarrow without trying to tie their tongues around *hemerocallis, perovskia,* or *achillea.* But in some cases, especially when you're talking about a genus with a whole bunch of species, and you need to get specific about which one, the only way is to use Latin. There are hundreds of varieties of *penstemon,* for example. These lovely western wildflowers, commonly called beardtongue (yuck), range from tall scarlet *Penstemon barbatus* to mat-forming blue *Penstemon virens.* Then there's pretty orange *P. pinifolius,* lovely pink *P. palmeri,* and wispy white *P. ambiguas.* If you get into penstemons, you gotta speak the lingo.

When it comes to pronunciation, don't stress. Latin is a dead language. It's nobody's native tongue. Do your best with this cumbersome old language. And if someone dares to correct your pronunciation of a name, just stare him or her down coolly and say, "Oh, that's the way I used to say it." This implies that you have been hanging out with more knowledgeable gardeners than they have and you must obviously be right.

Sort out the easy mispronunciations before you go to the nursery so you don't have them snickering behind your back. *Cotoneaster* is "ka-tone-ee-aster" not "cotton Easter." I'd say flowering tobacco for *nicotiana,* but if you must, pronounce it "ni-coh-she-anna" not "nikko-teen-a." Avoid *aquilegia* ("ah-qui-lee-ja" not "a-quill-a-gee-a"), and just say columbine instead.

■ Plant Types

TREES: GARDEN ELDERS

All this talk of sites, soils, and climates brings us to the basic business of knowing and growing plants. Plants have evolved to fill niches created by geography and topography. Trees tower above everything (sort of like carnivores on the food chain). They're tough and long-lived. Any tree planted today will, with care, likely outlive any of us, so its placement is the most critical of any plant you put in the soil. Trees need space. With their specific needs varying by species, they need enough room between them and your house, each other, power lines, and features like that. In most cities, the office of forestry offers guidelines and regulations on tree planting. Street trees especially must be placed so as to not block sight lines at intersections or to interfere with power lines and street lights. If you get it wrong, some city employee will probably pay you a visit. Some kinds and types of trees are even forbidden because they are brittle and are prone to breaking under snow and ice or from wind, which endangers cars and passersby. Multistemmed trees such as redbuds or dogwoods are often prohibited for planting along streets since they can block the views at intersections. Most drivers can see around a single trunk tree adequately, but a big mass of foliage is dangerous.

**Breaks in the canopy of trees allows beds of perennials and ornamental grasses
to flourish in this well-conceived plan.**

Trees differ in many ways. Evergreens hold their leaves (called needles if the tree is a spruce, pine, fir, or cypress) throughout the year, while deciduous trees drop their leaves in fall and grow new ones in spring. In frost-free climates, some trees hold their leaves throughout the year, while others still go through a seasonal renewal. At least two kinds of "evergreen" tree, the larch and bald cypress, go dormant in fall and drop their needles. There's an infamous tale in my city of a park maintenance crew who, thinking that it had died, cut down a prized bald cypress that was just in the bald phase of its normal cycle.

All trees flower. Some do it in spectacular fashion, while others are barely noticed except by allergy sufferers. Bees and other insects usually pollinate trees with big, showy, and scented flowers, such as fruit trees. Most other trees rely on the wind to blow about their massive amounts of pollen, which is precisely why spring can be so miserable for some of us.

Most trees have a single main trunk, and most deciduous trees create an interlocking canopy of branches. Trunks of every tree should always be respected and protected. While appearing to be the strongest part of the tree, the trunk is also the most vulnerable. Just beneath the bark is the lifeline of the tree, called the cambium layer, the vascular system that supports the tree the way our veins and arteries support us. When bark is damaged, that damage is usually irreversible, and the limbs on that side of the tree will often die. Even something as insignificant as a weed whacker can damage or kill a tree.

Tree roots need respect and protection, too. Compaction of the soil above the roots is to be avoided as this suffocates them and inhibits their ability to absorb water. The roots that do most of the work of searching for food and water, called feeder roots, are usually at and beyond the shady circle cast by the tree at high noon. This is called the drip line, because rain splashes from leaf to leaf, keeping the area directly beneath relatively dry. Remember that it doesn't do much good to water a tree right at the trunk since its feeder roots are many feet away.

WOODY PLANTS: SPACE AND CARE

Trees are durable because they're made of wood. This is either patently obvious or extremely profound, but I thought it needed to be said. Other woody plants—call them shrubs or bushes, it doesn't matter—are structured like trees. They can also be deciduous or evergreen, but their main similarity is their strong, woody constitution. All the considerations you give to a tree in placement and care apply to shrubs. One of the chronic mistakes that plague American gardeners is to crowd shrubs and not give them enough room to develop. This leads to much whacking and hacking, resulting in distorted, weird-looking bushes, often represented by the classic "light bulb" trim job. I know you've seen it. You've probably also driven past houses that have almost completely disappeared behind rampaging junipers whose growth habits the owners underestimated. There's a hilarious example in my neighborhood where the people neglected to read the tags when they planted cone-shaped junipers in front of their picture windows. Eventually, the view disappeared as the trees grew higher than the house. The owners then decided to trim all the branches below the roofline, leaving thick bare trunks with little "Christmas trees" perched upon them. I chuckle every time I drive by, but there's a lesson in that for all of us.

Most shrubs we grow in our gardens are either selected for their evergreen nature (often for winter interest) or for their flowers. A few, such as holly, are grown primarily for their handsome berries. Almost all flowering shrubs bloom on "old" wood, meaning only branches a year or more old will produce flowers. Keep in mind that if you do prune or trim (shrubs usually need much less grooming than we think), it should be done only right after they've finished blooming. Otherwise you'll be cutting off your next years' display.

ROSES: TENDER OR TOUGH

Roses are certainly the most popular of the shrubs. Novice gardeners want to grow them in the worst way. First-time rose growers envision huge bouquets of long-stemmed tea roses on their dining room tables. It's a nice dream, but those roses you received on Valentine's Day were greenhouse grown in supporting cages to keep their stems straight and long. And the bushes never experienced arctic winters or Saharan heat. Yours probably will.

Let's get realistic about roses. You'll have some for cutting, but don't get any ideas about opening your own flower shop. Wherever you garden, you can successfully grow hundreds of varieties of roses. Just don't get hung up on the hybrid teas at the beginning. Just as rewarding are the old-fashioned shrub roses, climbers, floribundas, and the so-called landscape roses and carpet roses. Most thrive with a minimum of care and some are even drought tolerant.

Shrub roses say romance in the garden. With their graceful, arching canes laden with sweet blooms, they conjure nostalgic visions of castles and cottages. Superb performers, they seldom, if ever, suffer from pests or diseases beyond an aphid or two (easily dispatched with a soapy spray). Widely grown across much of the nation are the classic early bloomers such as 'Persian

Yellow', 'Austrian Copper', and 'Harrison's Yellow'. The red-leaf rose, *Rosa glauca*, takes the prize as the most adaptable shrub rose. It will thrive in conditions from sun to part shade, clay to sand, and wet to dry. Pretty little single pink flowers grace the unusual leaves, blue-gray on top with maroon red underneath.

These large shrub roses can often be found in older neighborhoods where they put on spectacular early displays. Young shrub roses are like gawky teenagers, irregular and awkward looking. Give them space and time to fulfill their promise. Some people avoid planting these classics because they bloom only once each season. That's unfair. After all, I've never heard anyone complain because his or her lilacs, tulips, or lilies bloom only once a year.

Some shrub roses do bloom persistently, even in heat. The *rugosa* hybrids are simply wonderful. If I had to choose just one, it would be 'Therese Bugnet' (pronounced "boon-yay"). On bushes 4' by 5', its glossy green foliage supports full, pink flowers with the perfect "old rose" perfume. I'm also entranced by 'Golden Wings', an upright shrub type that grows to 4' or 5' tall. Its huge, single amber yellow flowers are accented by orange stamens and carry a soft fragrance. For an arbor or trellis, the classic ruby red 'Blaze' can't be beat, while pale pink 'New Dawn' is the stuff of fairy tales. Speaking of which, 'The Fairy' is a dainty but tough little shrub about 3' by 3' with nonstop clusters of satin pink blooms. It's beautiful with lavender or catmint as a "skirt" (most roses are lovely coupled with these plants). All these roses grow well in most regions, but there are certainly regional favorites that you can visit at local municipal gardens. Look

> **Wherever you garden, you can successfully grow hundreds of varieties of roses.**

Adobe-toned yarrow and a flurry of snow daisies enhance the much-admired classic hybrid tea rose 'Peace.'

Vines are really just shrubs with a posture problem.

for ones that demonstrate unusual vigor and clean, disease-free leaves. Also keep in mind how much room you want to devote to each bush. Can you accommodate the big boys, or are you best with the little guys?

Other compact varieties that perform tirelessly are the Meidiland series in white, coral, reds, and pinks. Easy and prolific, their single or double flowers fit in effortlessly with perennials such as meadow sage, pincushion flowers, catmints, snow daisies, and yarrow. Most roses—to my mind—look their best planted informally rather than regimented in rows. Hybrid tea roses benefit enormously when surrounded by casual companions that enhance their charms and disguise their weaknesses. To keep the advice short and sweet: plant roses in sun, keep them evenly moist, feed regularly, and prune in spring. I'm fond of a number of hybrid tea roses, but my favorite is the elegant cream and pink 'Peace'. This classic rose, bred in France just before World War II, survived because its breeder shipped a single cutting to a friend in America just before the Nazis invaded. The rest of the roses were destroyed, but 'Peace' endured. Just one of its flowers, floating in a bowl, is all any rose lover needs.

VINES: BEAUTIFUL CLIMBERS

Vines are really just shrubs with a posture problem. They've found a special niche in nature where they rely on their neighbors for support. The ultimate in social climbers, they cling and twine their way to ever-greater heights. Since they are lovely, we forgive them and give them fences, arbors, and trellises on which to grow and flower. Some enchant us with their flowers—clematis, honeysuckle, and wisteria—and others with their foliage—ivy and Virginia creeper. Grapes mean jelly, juice, and wine, and hops are a vital ingredient in beer. I've never made homemade wine or beer, but both grapes and hops make beautiful, albeit rambunctious, additions to the garden. A few very popular vines, such as morning glories and sweet peas, grow, flower, and die in one season, which makes them annuals. We'll talk about them shortly.

A planting of roses and perennials, including pink lupines and white valerian, is peppered with annual bread seed poppies.

PERENNIALS: LASTING PLEASURES

Perennial plants have a completely different strategy for survival than trees and shrubs. When cold weather hits, they retreat underground and wait out winter with their root systems. They return "perennially" each spring. Don't confuse "perennial" with "immortal," however, as some

Annuals in concert—glowing pink 'First Love' dianthus scores with blue and white forms of mealy-cup sage.

perennials run their course in just a few years. Others live to a very old age, such as peonies and daylilies. Since about the last quarter of the twentieth century, most Americans have based the bulk of their gardens around perennials. Just as hemlines go up and down and lapels go wide and then skinny, gardens go through periods of what's in and out. At the moment and for the foreseeable future, perennials figure prominently in most gardens. With trees and shrubs as the backdrop and structure of the garden, perennials take center stage. They're valued for their diversity, toughness, longevity, and—above all—beauty. A wonderful trend in American gardening today is to value every sort of plant and use it to best advantage. While Victorians didn't have much use for perennials, preferring showy, hothouse-raised annuals, we've come to embrace all kinds of plants regardless of their life cycles.

ANNUALS: COLORFUL ADDITIONS

When we picture annuals, we think of those vibrant, tempting flowers bursting out of their six-packs every spring at garden centers, supermarkets, and home improvement stores. These are the plants we rely on for continuous color all summer long. Usually grown from seed, annuals germinate, grow, flower, set seed, and die in a single season. It's a short, but dazzling life cycle. What's considered an annual depends on where you live. In most northern climates, the annual section includes many tender tropical and subtropical perennials, such as geraniums, that aren't hardy below freezing. My sister in Florida has geraniums older than her ancient cat. So in this category, we're including plants with a single-season life cycle in whichever climate you garden. Your local nursery can help you sort it all out. Many gardeners in cold-winter climates move these tender perennials indoors to save them from year to year.

Most annuals come packaged in handy six-packs or four-packs, but for the impatient, many garden centers offer mature blooming annuals in quart- or gallon-size pots. These, of course, come with higher price tags, but presumably are worth it for those who want instant gratification. A number of annuals aren't very suitable for six-packs, and grow best if sown directly in the ground. You'll save money as well as expand your selection if you learn to grow plants from seed. To build your confidence, start with the easy ones like sunflowers and marigolds.

Annuals prove themselves invaluable in a new garden because they grow to full size quickly. While everything else—trees, shrubs, and perennials—put down roots for the long haul, annuals fill the gaps and encourage the new gardener. But they're much more than gap-fillers. Even as the rest of the garden takes off, leave room for the gorgeous gaiety that annuals provide. I'd never want to go through a season without the brilliant blossoms of California poppies, moss roses, larkspurs, zinnias, or salvias. Annuals truly shine in container gardens as well. As mentioned previously, several vines are annual in nature. Among the most popular are morning glories, sweet peas, hyacinth beans, sweet potato vines, canary creepers, and climbing nasturtiums, not to mention peas and pole beans.

Many annuals that find your garden to their liking may respond by sowing themselves from year to year, making a one-time investment in them a very good one indeed. These "volunteers" can be thinned and transplanted to suit you. Johnny-jump-ups, larkspurs, bachelor's buttons, sweet alyssum, and several kinds of poppy—California, Shirley, corn, and lettuce-leaf—likely will form colonies in your garden. Count yourself lucky.

The care of annuals is as diverse as the plants themselves. Some like constant attention with lots of water and fertilizer. Some prefer benign neglect. Morning glories, cosmos, and nasturtiums—if fed and watered too much—will reward you with jungle-like growth, but deny you their flowers. It's called too much of a good thing.

BULBS: SPRING AND FALL

Bulbs take their preservation to extremes. Spring-flowering bulbs such as tulips and daffodils bide their wintertime underground, plumping themselves up with moisture. As winter retreats, the flowers of the bulb emerge. Sometimes they're a bit ahead of schedule and get caught by late freezes and snowstorms. Don't stress about your tulips, hyacinths, crocuses, daffodils, or snowdrops. They've evolved to bloom at that tricky time when winter and spring wrestle for dominance. They can withstand frost and snow (even if some flower stems snap). If they couldn't, they'd be extinct. If a heavy, wet snow threatens your tulips at the height of perfection, by all means cover them with bushel baskets, buckets, card tables, or whatever sheltering device you have handy. But these early bulbs don't need a blanket to keep them warm; they grow and flower best during the cool, sunny days of spring.

LEFT: Fall-blooming crocus belie the season with their springlike charms, contrasted by reddening plumbago foliage. RIGHT: Late spring-blooming Dutch iris pair attractively with variegated dogwood.

When things heat up, the spring bulbs finish their annual cycle by setting seed, soaking up the sun to provide energy for the next spring, and going through their ugly phase of unkempt, yellowing leaves. The best thing you can do is snap off their seedpods so they don't waste the energy, fertilize the plants to ensure a great display next spring, and ignore the yellowing leaves until they've turned brown. If you cut or pull off the foliage prematurely, you'll likely affect the bulb's ability to turn in a star performance next season. Live with it. By planting the bulbs farther back in beds—rather than right at the edge—emerging perennials will help camouflage the dying bulb leaves.

Summer doesn't spell the end of bulbs. Some even bloom in fall. The term bulb, by the way, refers to the enlarged roots that have evolved over time for each kind of bulbous plant. Some are categorized as true bulbs (tulips and lilies), some as corms (crocuses and gladiolus), some as rhizomes (irises), and others as tubers (dahlias). They all vary in shape and size, but they are all efficient storage containers. And the great thing is that they can sit dormant for months while they zip around the world, arriving at planting time at your neighborhood nursery. Then these hard brown chunks get buried, send out roots, plump up, and emerge above ground to grow and flower. I've always found that wondrous and wonderful.

The summer bulbs may be either hardy or tender, depending, once again, on where you garden. For most people, lilies, irises, and liatris can be treated as perennials. The rest of them—dahlias, cannas, elephant ears, caladiums, and gladiolus—must be dug after frost and their bulbs, corms, rhizomes, and tubers stored over winter.

Startling Flanders poppies seed themselves among an easy-care collection of classic bearded iris that are cut back and divided every four or five years.

I must warn you here about falling into a very bad habit concerning bearded iris. I adore these plants, so I feel protective toward them. Anyway, irises grow quickly, and to keep them healthy and blooming, you need to divide them every four or five years. After they flower in late spring, you dig up a clump and break up the rhizomes into pieces about six inches long with a single "fan" of leaves. You replant each fan right near the soil surface with 6" to 8" between each piece. Now here's the important part: Because the rhizome has a lot of work to do in getting its roots reestablished, you help out by cutting the fan of leaves down by half with scissors. The roots can't support all that top growth. If you follow these directions, you'll grow superb iris. However, never cut back the foliage unless you're transplanting the iris. For some odd reason, millions of Americans think they should go out after these bloom and punish their iris for a job well done by disfiguring the leaves and cutting off half of their system of making food. If I see you've done it, I'll knock on your door and give you a stern lecture. I travel extensively, so don't think you're safe just because you live in Salt Lake City or Sheboygan.

Summer- and autumn-flowering bulbs make amazing contributions to the garden and patio pots. I'm especially fond of cannas, lilies, and dahlias in big pots as exotic, colorful exclamation points on terraces and patios. Often overlooked, fall-blooming bulbs add enchantment to our gardens late in the season. Put a note in your daytimer to buy and plant them in late summer and early fall. It's worth the effort. Fall crocuses bring a touch of spring to our beds and borders even as the backdrop changes to yellow and bronze. Springing from the earth without leaves, these pretty flowers are ideally planted in concert with low-growing ground cover perennials such as thyme, partridge feather, and plumbago. Unusual in their life cycles, these bulbs send up their leaves in spring, soak up the sun, and disappear until their surprise late performance.

HERBS: USEFUL AND BEAUTIFUL

It used to be that the only herbs most folks encountered were lavender in their soaps, some mint in their juleps, and perhaps some parsley garnishing their dinner plates. Thank goodness those days are gone. As we all hunger for a healthier, tastier diet, herbs have become invaluable in our kitchens. We find them in many facets of our lives, from the medicine cabinet to the bathtub and the linen closet. Many people classify herbs as the "useful plants," whether they're used for culinary, cosmetic, medicinal, or household purposes.

An herb garden can be a charming garden room. Alternately, herbs lend themselves to growing in borders or vegetable and cutting gardens as well as pots. One big misconception that you may have heard

> As we all hunger for a healthier, tastier diet, herbs have become invaluable in our kitchens.

An unusual "scare camel" protects a country garden that rivals those in southern France for charm, with its casual mix of lavender, daisies, poppies and ornamental onions.

repeated is that herbs like terrible soil and tough conditions. This, of course, depends on your soil type, but I guess it stems from the fact that many popular cooking herbs come from the Mediterranean region. Oregano, thyme, tarragon, rosemary, lavender, savory, and sage love full sun, don't need much water, and prosper in a mineral-rich, not-too-fluffed-up soil. To some people, that means poor soil; but for most of us, that's what we've got. Other herbs such as basil or ginger like organically rich, moist soil. Herbs display the same diversity as any other group of plants but, in general, are quite adaptable. Many that you wish to grow may thrive happily in a room devoted strictly to them. As you grow and experiment with this fascinating group, your kitchen and home will change forever.

TURF: WISE CARE

One of my summer chores growing up was tending the lawn. I hated it. But I learned what it took to have a healthy lawn with minimal effort (never underestimate an adolescent who'd rather be doing something else). Fertilize and aerate in spring and fall. Dig dandelions by hand the minute they start to bloom. Water during the coolest part of the day. And water infrequently and deeply to encourage the roots to delve deeply in search of water. Roots near the surface burn up. Set the mower blade at the highest level, the better to shade the roots during hot weather.

I've stood by these early findings ever since, and I've always had healthy, resilient lawns with a minimum of crabgrass (which I also hand-dig before it goes to seed) and never an instance of mold, fungus, or the other horrors that seem to plague overwatered grass. An inch of moisture a week is not only sufficient but also advisable for a tough turf that can roll with the punches. If you get moss in parts of your lawn, consider this: perhaps nature is telling you that moss would be more suitable than turf. Some of the most beautiful "lawns" I've seen in New England were made of moss.

I've recently reached a point in my life where I am lawn-free. The recent western drought pushed me over the edge. I don't begrudge anyone else's right to enjoy their lawn for family activities and, perhaps, the pleasure of tending it. Just do it responsibly and wisely to get the most out of your work and water. Many seasoned gardeners I know have little or no lawn. It all starts by expanding the borders by a foot or two. Sometimes a gardening couple will argue about whether this is necessary (husbands tend to treasure the time spent with their lawns), but eventually the border prevails.

As you plan your new garden, you may be starting with nothing more than a lawn. Ask yourself, "Do I really want that responsibility, to maintain a lawn up to the neighborhood standard?" It's work. Flower and vegetable gardening is work, too, but a lot less monotonous, and (in my opinion) infinitely more rewarding. Limiting the size of turf areas reduces water consumption and allows you to better care for what you've got. Eventually, I'd guess, you'll be nibbling away at the edges to make more room for flowers.

GROUND COVERS AND TURF ALTERNATIVES: ALONE OR TOGETHER

While various kinds of turf are the ultimate ground covers, a number of low-growing, low-maintenance perennials can serve much the same purpose. They're not suitable for badminton or dodgeball, but they offer a pretty alternative to the big stretch of green lawn. They're also

A tapestry of ground covers on a rocky slope includes sedums, snow-on-the-mountain, and ice plants, punctuated by flaming Oriental poppies.

---

ideal for slopes, hills, and irregular terrain that may be a challenge to mow. You can choose to plant a single ground cover, such as a moss or thyme. Or you can plant many kinds of ground covers as a tapestry of intertwining colors and textures. The best ground covers for your area will be found at your local nursery. Widely grown kinds include creeping veronica, thyme, brass button, ivy, lily turf (*Liriope*), pachysandra, lamium, vinca, wine cup, partridge feather, creeping baby's breath, mat daisy, Irish and Scottish moss, creeping phlox, hen and chicks, sedum, and ice plant. In addition, many require less water than most lawn grasses and little or no fertilization. And you never need to mow. Your world will become a quieter place.

■ Your Style

Never give up your vision. Style transcends climate. Almost everything is possible, budget and patience permitting. At the same time, consider the region in which you live and its natural landscape, as well as its signature plants—whether native (meaning indigenous) or not—that provide its gardening identity. After all, what's Portland without roses, Phoenix without saguaro cacti, New Orleans without bougainvillea vines, Richmond without dogwood trees, Denver without

Style transcends climate. Almost everything is possible, budget and patience permitting.

Southwestern gardeners draw on the desert and Native American cultures for inspiration, as strong architectural plants make a bold style statement.

blue spruce, or Washington, D.C., without cherry trees? The gardening heritage of your city or state may be an important factor in determining the style and contents of your garden.

The architecture of your home also figures into that determination. My modest turn-of-the-century cottage would look downright silly with a Louis XIV clipped ornamental garden, complete with formal pools and statuary. Conversely, a naturalistic meadow would appear equally out of place surrounding a stately brick Tudor home. We all borrow from other places and other times when conceiving our garden visions. Translating them into reality is what it's all about. For example, my garden is a hybrid between the classic perennial border garden and a cottage garden. Some might claim, "You can't do an English garden in Denver!" (or Kansas City or Charlotte or wherever you live). But they've disregarded the fact that any style of garden is simply that—a style. Had I planted mine with plants that thrive in England, I'd be doomed to failure. As it is, my English-themed garden has a Colorado twist, featuring flowers that survive and thrive in my dry, hot-in-summer, cold-in-winter climate. Plants don't know or care about style; they're satisfied when they get the right spot in the right garden.

■ Garden Rooms

Rooms organize a house. Most of us bathe in one room, cook in another, sleep, do laundry, play, read, and watch TV in others. Some rooms do double duty. Others don't do much. Unlike its namesake, for instance, the living room is often the least lived-in room in the house.

Rooms can also organize a garden (and they are really "living" rooms), even if they're not strictly for daily activities. When I'm in the garden, I'd just as soon ignore dirty dishes, piles of laundry, and the day's top stories. Time spent in a garden is unlike any other activity. Some days it's all about color and excitement. Others are about manicuring and attention to details. War is occasionally declared on weeds, while every once in awhile a day is dreamy and peaceful.

My garden is organized into several rooms. Some are for the pleasure and convenience of people, others for the specific requirements of the plants in them (shade, sun, moisture, etc.). As with the rooms of a house, these garden rooms demand care and attention. Like an interior designer who creates a room, I rarely get to use it the way it's intended. I'm more of a maid with dirty nails and knees. But that's my own fault: I've made my (garden) bed, now I must lie in it.

When friends come over, I'm forced to enjoy my garden. While I join in the conversation, music, and wine, however, I'm secretly thinking that the flowering maple over there is looking droopy and I've just got to get those bug-bitten leaves off the golden sweet potato vine. And that begonia really ought to be deadheaded. Right now! Pretty gardens do require time and the right kind of work at the right time. But perhaps the emphasis I've placed on the work involved to create one is misleading. It's not really work, after all, if it's something you enjoy. A garden is much more than a place in which to work. It's a place to live.

PLANNING A GARDEN ROOM

Let's focus on creating a garden room for a well-balanced, moderately industrious gardener. What do you plan to do in your garden room? In a conventional house, the activities are already assigned by room before we even move in. Their size, shape, fixtures, and location already determine how they're to be used. A stove or a tub is a good indicator. The rooms without appliances give us a little more wiggle room to turn them into something besides a spare bedroom, such as a library, sewing room, or home theater.

A garden room starts from scratch. At the start, the only thing that it has in common with an indoor room is a floor. In most cases, it has no walls, windows, ceilings, furniture, or ornaments. Sometimes, such as in the city, walls of other buildings define the garden space. New

**A former concrete patio slab has been transformed into a peaceful room—perfect for knitting—
with the addition of brick pavers, comfy wicker, and pots of blue lily-of-the-Nile.**

Yorkers know all about this. But many people simply have a "yard," which is usually the lawn, trees, and shrubs that surround the house. The closest most yards get to having a room is the patio, oftentimes a concrete afterthought tacked onto the back of the house.

A real garden room can serve as an extension of the home. Your lifestyle will help you decide how it should be designed, whether for dining, entertaining, catnapping, or all of the above. Creating one room leads to another. Any garden appears larger when it's segmented and all is not apparent at first glance. Other garden rooms can be simply for display, showcasing a collection of plants the way we display trophies, books, and figurines inside. Taking the concept of a room too literally, collectors sometimes find a way to clutter it up with non-plant items. Take the case of an elderly couple I once saw on British TV who collected more than 500 gnomes. The broadcast showed them demolishing their collection with sledgehammers. When asked why, the lady of the house replied, "It got to be a bit much, really." I'm sure there's a lesson for all of us in this.

Getting back to the business of creating a room, the only thing that is absolutely necessary is a sense of enclosure. This can start perhaps with a wall or walls of a building and include fences, pillars, planters, and screens as well as living elements such as hedges and potted plants. Most of us don't like to sit in a room without windows (except at the movies) so the enclosure doesn't need to be thorough. A garden room doesn't necessarily need a ceiling, but it becomes more intimate with some sort of canopy, whether it's a tree, arbor, pergola, or even an umbrella.

> I'd rather dine in a garden than in the fanciest restaurant in the world.

DINING IN THE GARDEN

When I picture creating a garden room, I think about food. I'd rather dine in a garden than in the fanciest restaurant in the world. For one thing, I'm already dressed for it. For another, a summer's evening breeze scented by lilies or angel's trumpets enhances any meal (even one I cook). But even great tastes and scents are secondary if you're uncomfortable, so consider what you and your guests will sit on for a meal in an outdoor dining room. Teak, wrought iron, and cast aluminum—they're all great choices, depending on your taste. I don't go in for plastic—it just doesn't fit in with any of my garden concepts—but because this type of furniture is inexpensive, you can use it initially until you can find and afford what you really like. Furniture makes a design statement in a garden dining room. Sometimes it says, "French café," "English tea time," "Southern elegance," or "Laguna Beach lunch." I'm not exactly sure what mine says except maybe, "This looks comfy," mainly due to cushions and pillows. I'm constantly shuttling them inside when rain clouds appear, but they help to set a mood.

Mood is what a garden room is all about. You create it. It's a room like no other, always changing. And what's even better, a little dirt is perfectly acceptable. Some of my favorite moments have been spent in my outdoor dining room, never mind my compulsive gardening and inability to relax. I recall chili on a cold day, a cool salad on a warm night, the excitement of planting containers each spring, and just hanging out with my pets. I love watching the cats stalk butterflies and the dogs snoozing under the table or "helping" me with watering and deadheading.

A garden room isn't just about entertaining and relaxing. I don't relax much in the vegetable and herb room. I sweat. There's a chair and table in the shade to take a break, but the focus here is production. Though some people integrate vegetables and herbs into the rest of the garden, many gardeners like a separate area dedicated to them. Or they put vegetables and flowers for cutting together (a cutting garden). Some of us just find it too difficult to pick from the garden for fear it would spoil the show. I'm reluctant to pick from my main borders, too.

■ Beds and Borders

Let's talk about beds and borders. What's the difference? There really isn't much. A bed is usually a flat patch of ground, often carved out of the lawn. Traditionally, it displays bright

Where no rules apply, annuals, perennials, and shrubs stuff beds (or are they borders?) carved informally from the lawn. The plantings include roses, lupines, black-eyed Susans, penstemons, and dianthus.

summer annuals, such as petunias and geraniums, commonly known as "bedding" plants. At one time, when Britannia ruled the waves and Queen Victoria sat on the throne of England, bedding was all the rage. You could show off your wealth based on how grand, intricate, and labor-intensive your garden beds were. We don't see much of this in home gardens any longer, but remnants of it linger in municipal parks every summer. Occasionally a town or city will spell out its name in marigolds, for example. A local hotel tried this a couple of years ago using petunias. It was fairly legible as you drove by in early summer, but as the petunias grew and spread, the hotel name became a blur. The Victorians had enormous gardening staffs to snip and clip. At any rate, we don't bed so much these days.

By contrast, we make borders. A border is largely a European concept, especially English, which replaces beds of annuals with beds of perennials. We'll talk about these kinds of plants in detail later in the book, but suffice it to say that perennials live for many years and come up "perennially" each year, while annuals usually live up to their name and must be planted anew each year. By the very word "border," you might imagine that this piece of ground borders something, such as a wall, walkway, or property line. It can, of course, border something, but it's come to mean an arrangement of perennials usually in long, rectangular expanses. My "borders" are really just two equal strips of earth about 60' by 10' with a path down the middle. Some people like lawns running down their borders or a layer of fine pea gravel that crunches as you walk. A border can run alongside a driveway or fence, go uphill if it has to, and it doesn't even have to be straight. Borders traditionally have some sort of backing to them such as a wall or hedge. A lot of the English ones employ romantically crumbling brick walls. Mine has a picket fence. Whatever it is, the backing serves as a sort of device like a picture frame to set off the beauty of the plants.

Though a border used to be strictly about perennials, it's come to include just about every kind of plant you'd like to toss in it. This "mixed border" concept is a boon to kitchen-sink gardeners like me who wish to incorporate roses, tulips, basil, and anything else we fancy.

The most important part about a border is its complete lack of regimentation. This means no rows and essentially no strict rules. A beautiful border does, however, need a bit of discipline both in its planning and maintenance to keep from looking chaotic. For that we'll discuss colors, shapes, textures, and the sequence of blooms—later.

You've probably heard about "cottage gardens" as much as borders. They're planted just about the same as borders, really, but I'd say that they're especially exuberant and expressive. A famous British garden writer once called cottage gardens "undisciplined masses of flopping vegetation." When they became all the rage, he wrote a glowing book about them. Most of us are essentially cottage gardeners when we start, and after years of experimentation—becoming increasingly sophisticated—we often return to our cottage roots. I used to care far more about clever combinations. Last summer, I accidentally grew a blood red dahlia in a pot with magenta petunias, chartreuse sweet potato vine, and orange cigar plant. It was absolutely hideous and I didn't give a hoot. I'm definitely back to my exuberant cottage phase.

> Most of us are essentially cottage gardeners when we start, and after years of experimentation—becoming increasingly sophisticated—we often return to our cottage roots.

■ Rocks in the Garden

Rock gardeners are just cottage gardeners with rocks. They specialize in smaller plants, often from mountainous areas, that grow best amongst rocks, especially in the crevices. Rock gardeners almost always display meticulous grooming techniques as well as a huge thirst to try new plants. Gardening with rocks is a bit different than pure rock gardening. Many people garden with natural rock formations on their properties. Others haul in rocks to pay homage to the natural landscape of their regions.

My sister and I did this—in our own ways—when we were kids. On family trips to the mountains, we were allowed to bring home rocks we collected. Betty and I managed some fairly large-sized rocks that we put in the back of our family station wagon. We saved those for our rock gardens, which we planted with creeping phlox and hen and chicks and populated with

**Stone, wood, and water characterize a Japanese-inspired garden,
with breathtaking water lilies inviting reflection.**

our pet turtles. My sister and I built rock gardens all over the place. It's great to have gardening parents who don't worry about what the neighbors think of their children's latest creation.

Japanese and Chinese styles of gardens often employ rocks in their designs, but for entirely different reasons than creating plant habitats. Many gardeners enjoy bringing Asian elements into their home gardens, as well as evoking the styles of planting. Stone, wood, and water can be used in many ways to evoke an Asian look. One word of caution: the architecture of your home must lend itself to these styles. Simplicity of line and ornament is critical to do justice to your interpretation of a Japanese garden surrounding your home. My understanding is that Japanese gardens, in particular, serve as artistic microcosms of the natural world. Before you do a sand garden or throw up a teahouse, investigate this discipline of gardening thoroughly. As with European styles of gardening, use plants suitable to your region in an Asian-inspired garden.

■ Naturalistic Gardens

Wherever you live, you'll find gardens that mirror the natural landscape. One of the strongest garden movements today is about prairies, plains, and meadows. There aren't many left of the virgin grasslands that used to cover so much of this continent. Cornfields and pastures have largely supplanted the plains. I have a particular appreciation for the plants I grew up with on the plains. From the edge of town where we lived, an endless sea of grasses stretched to the horizon.

Prairie and meadow gardens strive to present the beauty of these habitats. Besides the predominant grasses, these gardens also feature many of the wildflowers that, because of their toughness and beauty, have become garden stalwarts throughout the world, such as Indian blanket, goldenrod, aster, gayfeather, and coreopsis.

Most flowers were once wild, except for those "bred in captivity." Through breeding and selection, plants from around the world have blossomed into the ones that we grow in our gardens today. Hybrid tea roses, for example, aren't to be found just growing down by the side of the ditch. As "wild" subjects, many forerunners of modern hybrids look quite different. Modern dahlias, zinnias, and marigolds (all native to Mexico) have become big, bold, and brassy in comparison to the original wild plants. For many gardeners, the charm of the originals far outweighs the "improvements" by breeders.

These are what we usually think of when we picture wildflowers. They vary from region to region, of course, with some having a very large range and others being quite localized. Many

A rustic fence is all that separates these "captive" columbines from the untamed woods beyond; seedlings will likely jump the fence in the coming years.

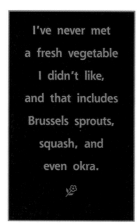

I've never met a fresh vegetable I didn't like, and that includes Brussels sprouts, squash, and even okra.

gardeners enjoy going "native," planting and growing the wild species of their regions. Already adapted to your soil and climate, they will probably prove to be tough and enduring.

■ Garden Edibles

Despite the fact that this introduction to gardening does not focus on edible plants, I wanted to be sure to offer a few tips to those of you who will not be content with a strictly ornamental garden. Growing up in a gardening family gave me an appreciation for working in the soil, even at a very early age, and for more than just growing plants. I also liked hoeing rows, planting seeds, and especially harvesting. Kids are notoriously fussy about eating vegetables (and often turn into fussy adults). But children in gardening families never need to be prodded to eat their peas, beets, or beans.

I've never met a fresh vegetable I didn't like, and that includes Brussels sprouts, squash, and even okra. I salivate just writing about homegrown corn and tomatoes. The popularity of farmer's markets testifies to our appreciation of freshly picked vegetables. As soon as a vegetable is picked, its sugar begins to turn to starch and the flavor fades. Carrots, corn, and peas are decidedly more delicious if eaten straight from the garden (or, in my case, in the garden; peas rarely make it to the kitchen).

Taste isn't the only reason to raise your own vegetables. With the tremendous popularity of pesticide-free, organically grown produce, it makes sense to raise your own healthy crops. The key is not to panic at the arrival of the first aphid. You can manage outbreaks of pests using soap. That's right, soap. Pure garden soap that you mix with water is available at garden centers. It doesn't poison insects, but instead dissolves their hard exoskeletons. Like the Wicked Witch of the West, they melt away. Explain that to your kids and they'll be thrilled to help spray the soap.

While pests are always a cause of concern, the most important aspect of growing vegetables is your soil. Although a loose, friable (crumbly) soil is ideal, a lack of it doesn't mean you're out of luck. Homeowners with heavy clay soil and high-rise dwellers without any soil at all have options. Raised beds filled with fertile topsoil can be created, and heavy soils can be improved by incorporating organic matter. And almost anybody with a balcony that receives at least a half-day's sun can grow vegetables in containers.

Root crops such as beets, turnips, carrots, onions, and radishes grow best in very loose soil with the consistency of store-bought potting soil. They have a difficult time extending their roots into heavy or rocky soil. Raised beds and large containers provide that ideal, loose growing medium.

As you plan your vegetable garden, choose a spot that receives plenty of sun. Some people don't consider a vegetable garden very pretty and hide it behind the garage or along the alley. Don't fall into that trap. Find the best spot for growing vegetables and turn it into a beautiful space. It can hold its own as a viable garden room if you enclose it with nice fencing or hedges, dress it up with ornaments such as a birdbath (birds should always be welcome to dine on insects), and create an interesting layout with paths and paving. Trellises and arbors add further architectural interest and support climbers such as pole beans, peas, and squash. Many gardeners add flowers to their vegetable garden, especially edible ones such as pansies, nasturtiums, and sweet Williams.

Vegetables are split into two groups: cool-season and warm-season. At the beginning of the growing season (cool season), depending on where you live, you can plant seeds or transplant young nursery seedlings of lettuce, spinach, peas, beets, radishes, and onions. They can withstand a light frost—even snow—and develop rapidly during cool, sunny weather. When the real heat hits (warm season), spinach and lettuce will bolt (send up flowering stalks), and their usefulness is over. Radishes become bitter and woody and peas cease flowering and become magnets for spider mites. Pull up these cool-season plants and compost them, and plant heat-loving vegetables in their place. Warm soil is essential for beans, corn, and squash to germinate well.

More tomatoes succumb to bad judgment about timing than any other crop. Peppers are right up there, too. Don't jump the gun: One unseasonably hot day doesn't mean it's safe to plant your warm-season crops. Tomatoes and peppers grow so quickly that even those planted in early June in northern gardens and in mountainous areas will rapidly catch up and soon surpass plants set out too early. Neither can stand one degree below freezing, and cool nights will stunt their growth for the entire season. Pay attention to the night temperatures in your area—they must stay reliably above 50 degrees; daily highs are irrelevant.

My best tip for growing great tomatoes (the favorite of most gardeners) is to bury a young transplant all the way up to its set of lower leaves. Tomatoes root all along the stem this way, ensuring a sturdy, well-rooted plant. Keep the soil evenly moist, feed regularly with a fertilizer formulated especially for tomatoes, and pick and stomp pesky tomato hornworms. Nothing beats the taste of a homegrown tomato. Each bite is memorable. I can almost taste it now.

■ Container Gardening

For everything you want to grow but don't think you can, there's container gardening. You control the soil, fertilizer, and water to accommodate most any plant you've been hankering to grow. The 300 pots on my patio and balcony are a testament to a lot of hankering.

Start with large pots of at least 10" or 12" diameters. Any smaller and you'll never be able to keep the soil within them moist (my small pots get good use housing my collection of succulents and cactus, which don't need much water). Terra-cotta pots "breathe," meaning that their porous walls allow both air and moisture to penetrate the walls. While that's beneficial to roots, it's not so good if the pots dry out on a hot day when you're not home. Containers made of fiberglass, wood, plastic, and glazed pottery don't breathe and consequently hold moisture better. Use potting soil (bags of commercially available soil labeled "potting soil" can be found at any nursery or garden supply store); garden soil rarely makes a suitable growing medium in pots.

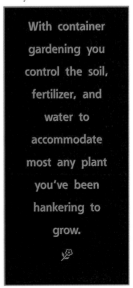

With container gardening you control the soil, fertilizer, and water to accommodate most any plant you've been hankering to grow.

You can create beautiful combinations of plants by blending upright, rounded, and trailing plants for a balanced effect. Plant them very tightly together for a lush look right off the bat. Fertilize every week to ten days to get great "magazine cover" results. Some plants may be best grown as single specimens in their own pots. They can then be grouped with other pots. I use bricks, blocks, and overturned pots beneath my

A low stone wall elevates pots of flowers for an up-close experience, including oxalis, pink spider lily, pale pink Asiatic lilies, magenta stock, and white alstroemeria.

containers to stage them for the best show. I try to get many of them up to eye level so I can enjoy them when I'm dining or writing. Conversely, lower your hanging baskets so you're not just staring at the bottom of the basket.

Individual pots or groupings of them serve as focal points in the garden, disguise eyesores, direct traffic flow, provide screening, and mainly beautify our outdoor living spaces. Though we think of container plantings essentially for summer color, they're useful anytime, not only in frost-free climates but in cold ones as well. Holly, evergreens, and ornamental grasses can be especially attractive with a light dusting of snow. Also, containers can host dwarf fruit trees, evergreens, flowering shrubs, bulbs, and almost everything else that is ordinarily grown in the ground. (Rooftop and balcony gardeners need big pots and planters for some of these options.)

■ Watery Effects

A pond, reflecting pool, or fountain serves as cooling relief from summer's heat and glare. Gardeners' ponds play a vital role for birds, both for drinking and bathing. Even if you have no intention of ever installing a water feature in your garden, at least provide a bowl of clean water. The birds will revel in it and repay you by eating your unwanted insects.

When you do take the plunge and become a water gardener, you'll enter an exciting new world with its own lingo. Soon, you'll talk liners, pumps, filters, fish, and algae like a pro. You'll fall in love with water lilies and my favorite, the lotus. With its graceful blue-green leaves and elegant pink flowers, it's no wonder the lotus was used by ancient Egyptians as a recurring artistic motif.

Beyond water lilies and lotus, a pond may host many beautiful aquatics, especially those plants that thrive at water's edge. Some are hardy and may be planted directly in the mucky soil where their roots stay perpetually wet, while others are kept in their pots and submerged below water level. Among the loveliest of these plants are Japanese and Louisiana irises as well as *Iris pseuda-corus*, the fabled yellow fleur-de-lis of France. Rushes, reeds, and cattails are also perfect for the water's edge, along with tropical elephant ears (*Colocasia*), pickerel, papyrus, and water cannas. The dramatic foliage of rodgersias and ligularias can be stunning, topped by pink or golden flowers, respectively. Some water plants simply float. Water hyacinth, water lettuce, and duckweed migrate around the pond with the breeze. The first two should only be allowed in enclosed ponds, as they have become major pests in the South, escaping into and clogging waterways.

Deciding what sort of water feature you want is the most important part. It takes a deft touch to pull off a naturalistic pond. Unless you have a lot of space (in full sun, by the way), it's difficult to make your pond convincing. How many of us city dwellers have a natural spring and a rock outcropping in our backyards? In the country or where there are hills and rock formations, the illusion is far more convincing, but a more formal approach may work best for most of us.

A convincingly naturalistic pond teems with life such as an orange canna, rushes, water lilies, and golden yellow ligularia.

My raised pond, about 4' by 8', doesn't pretend to be natural. It has provided me with hours of entertainment as well as some strange encounters. You may meet some big birds. Herons may come for a tasty meal. A light on your pond at night is the equivalent of the famed golden arches to night-flying herons. Some water gardeners resort to netting over their ponds, but the best idea comes from my friends Susan and Rhonda, who bought black plastic boxes (about the size of a bread box) at a home improvement store. The boxes, intended for some sort of plumbing, have holes for tubes and pipes so the fish can swim in and out and hide inside. It works like a charm.

Raccoons regularly mug my pond. Whether it's to wash or eat (there always seem to be fewer fish after one of their visits), they just trash my pond. I put mousetraps on the pond's edge to deter them. The fish population seems to rebound from the predations and only once have I needed to start from scratch. Several winters ago, a warm day lured my goldfish to the surface. The temperature plunged suddenly, trapping them in the ice. This is known as the "great fish stick episode." The adventure continues.

■ Color Basics

We've talked plenty about plants, although barely mentioning what draws us to them: color. We're all so different. And we see color differently. Some of us are cautious or confused about color. Others, like me, tend to collect one or two kinds of plants and give scant thought to color combinations. Then there are the magpies, who are attracted to bright, shiny objects, and have one of everything. There are also the minimalists, whose color palette is extremely limited. And finally, there are those with a "survival garden," where the color scheme is based on what hasn't died.

Unfortunately, too many of us never find out what we really like because we're scared to experiment. Whether it's our home, wardrobe, or garden, we're so unsure and afraid of making mistakes that we limit ourselves before we even start. Many people stick with the equivalent of a black cocktail dress. They play it safe.

Comparing colors of apparel and garden flowers isn't quite fair, but I think people confuse

To begin experimenting with color, take one base color and repeat it over and over in your plantings.

them. You have no idea how many times I've heard a client say, "I hate orange," or "I loathe yellow." It's too bad that somewhere between our first box of crayons and adulthood we learned to hate a particular color. I have to respect this prejudice, of course, but on what is it based? If it's because you look hideous in yellow or orange, don't wear it. Clothing is next to our skin and hair; flowers bloom against a green background.

Coats of color paint the garden throughout the season. Planning helps to match them with the appropriate time. Our psychological needs should be considered in the process. In northern states, for example, gardeners are hungry—no, ravenous—for spring color after a monochromatic winter. In summer, blues and lavenders provide a slight respite from the heat. And in fall, gold and orange match our moods, even if they might seem out of sync at any other time. There's no reason to exclude any color from the garden; just find the season where it best fits.

The palette of spring plantings can be among the weirdest. Maybe it's because the fall-planted bulbs aren't ever compared with the perennials with which they'll bloom until they erupt into a big spring clash. After all, a tulip is just a picture on a bag when we plant it. Small wonder that some combinations are excessively cheerful. Red tulips and basket-of-gold are the visual equivalents of nails on a chalkboard to me. Yellow daffodils and hot pink creeping phlox I find equally disturbing. I actually like this perennial and employ it frequently, especially soft pink 'Candy Stripe' and 'Emerald Blue', although the latter is so deceivingly named. Its color is delicate lavender-blue. (The color peacemakers in the garden are blue, purple, or lavender.) I've usually found that almost all pastels go together without much trouble and that all intense colors—let's call them jewel tones—work well together.

Because color can be so personal and so emotional, I don't believe in assigning rules about it. Even if I did, I also believe that rules are for breaking. There are some tips, however,

Pretty in pink, these Asiatic lilies, pincushion flowers, and rose campion get a boost from the chartreuse leaves of variegated yucca and golden hops vine.

that can help a bit when approaching color. To begin experimenting with color, take one base color and repeat it over and over in your plantings. This is similar to painting the walls of a room with a consistent color. Since we were discussing lavender-blue anyway, consider how soothing it is and how many perennials and shrubs feature lavender-blue flowers, from veronicas and catmints to salvias and butterfly bushes. This color can span the seasons, providing a base for adding bolder jewel tones.

The same base color could be pink, yellow, or white. Then you can go off in any direction that suits you and the season. In the case of lavender-blue, add some deeper blues and purples and you've set the stage for hot pink or coral accents, or perhaps even orange. Oddly enough, if you take the base colors of pink, yellow, or white and add darker blues and purples, you've set up exactly the same situation. A base color plus purple is the ideal way to incorporate jewel tones into the garden, whether they're golden California poppies, ruby roses, magenta wine cups (*Callirhoe involucrata*), or orange tiger lilies.

The base color idea is also practical for those who collect plants that span a wide color range, such as irises or lilies. Sometimes these flowers come in unusual shades—or several at one time—that are a bit hard to fit in gracefully. A simple base color background pulls it all together. For the magpie gardeners, who are attracted to bright colors and pick up one of this and one of that until their gardens look like button collections, add a base color to make some semblance of order out of the hodgepodge. This could be as simple as broadcasting (i.e., spreading) a half pound of bachelor's buttons or sweet alyssum seeds (in a single color, not a mix) to fill in the gaps and provide unity.

Minimalist schemes are often great experiments—in the beginning. If you create a garden room that's limited in color (and you become as tired of it as I became of my all-white border), try adding the equivalent of throw pillows. Toss in one new color each season—even if it's just a foliage contrast—such as lime green in an all-yellow garden or burgundy in all-pink or -red one.

Finally—and you know who you are—there are those with a color scheme based on what's left from what you planted last year. Plenty of gardens start out with lovely color schemes, but the voles ate the tulips, the daisies croaked last winter, and the astilbe succumbed during the drought. What's left doesn't hang together. I've seen living rooms like this too. The walls used to match the sofa that the cat shredded, and the new chintz chairs were such a great deal, even though they're not that great with the plaid upholstery on the new sofa.

Let's make it simple. Pick one accent foliage color, such as silver, and three colors (make one of them bright) say pale pink, powder blue, and magenta. If you've already planted, dig out everything that doesn't fit this scheme and give these strays to your neighbors. Go to the nursery. Splurge.

■ Think Ahead When Buying

Keep in mind that summer and fall flowers are not in bloom in spring; two-thirds of your purchases should be for coming seasons. Spring may seem like an odd time to plan for fall color in the garden, but each autumn we do the reverse, planting crocuses, daffodils, and tulips to greet us in spring. It makes sense to take advantage of our early-season enthusiasm to ensure a colorful garden late in the year.

Summer heat often puts a damper on planting. If it's hot and/or dry, it's both tiring and risky to plant perennials. And let's face it: We buy what's in bloom. Most people purchase their plants in spring. Blooming annuals and perennials fly off the garden center shelves. The gallon pots of later-blooming perennials, devoid of bloom, get passed by. If you truly want a profusion of bloom throughout the season, a full half of your spring purchases should be strictly green. That's right, no flowers. To do this, you need to do some homework. What late bloomers are suitable for your garden?

People who need instant gratification will need to steel themselves. It's difficult to resist color. If you buy smart, your garden will be as beautiful in September as in June, if not more so. Don't forget the crescendo effect: by combining annuals with late-blooming perennials, the color will intensify throughout the summer and into fall. Many annuals reach their peaks in late August and September, coinciding with the explosion of fall-blooming perennials. Annual zinnias, dahlias, gomphrenas, verbenas, sweet potato vines, and black-eyed Susans hit their stride just as perennial asters, mums, hummingbird trumpets, plumbagos, coneflowers, Japanese anemones, and ornamental grasses come into their own.

Planting late bloomers in spring gives them almost an entire season to grow and perform. Even small-sized plants, with proper care, can put on a great show, although they'll be even more amazing in coming years. There's an old saying about perennials: "The first year they sleep, the second year they creep, the third year they leap." They may leap a little faster than the old adage—depending on the attention and fertilizer you lavish upon them—but have patience for a year or two.

■ Weed Strategies

Dreams do come true in fairy tales (and sometimes in gardens), but it's usually after plenty of toil and suffering. In fairy tales, the usual cause of all the turmoil is the wicked stepmother. In gardens, it's the weeds. During the excitement of planning and planting, weeds aren't on our minds. We're dreaming of tulips and roses and tomatoes. How dare weeds give us a wake-up call?!

Everyone wants a magic "cure" for weeds. For the kind of garden I like and design, there isn't one. I don't use or recommend black plastic, landscape fabric, weed barrier cloth, or smothering bark nuggets. They're just not natural. The only way to achieve a real garden is with real sweat. And that means weeding.

Weeds are a fact of life. Whenever we turn a spadeful of earth, we're exposing opportunistic seeds. Developing a strategy for coping with them is part of making a new garden or enlarging an existing one. In one category are the really bad, horrible weeds. Whoever said that a weed is just a flower growing in the wrong spot must have been on heavy medication or never ran into the likes of bindweed, kudzu, bittersweet, thistle, and various ivies. You probably know about the worst thugs in your neighborhood. They're basically despised for their aggression, tenacity, and deep roots. In the other category are the pesky weeds, slightly less aggravating because of their annual nature. These include portulaca, wild lettuce, shepherd's purse, mare's tail, lamb's quarters, hen bit, dandelion, pigweed, and knotweed. It's funny that so many carry picturesque—even cute—common names. Their greatest strength is in their numbers—kajillions of them.

I've never had the good fortune to start one of my own gardens on a piece of property that didn't host a couple of really bad thugs. Sometimes they've even fooled me into thinking I'd conquered them, only to discover they were just waiting until I'd planted before rearing their ugly heads again. My best piece of advice is to make sure they're good and dead before you plant. The method of killing them is up to you and depends on the nature of the villains.

The worst possible thing to do is to rototill if you're facing a persistent, deep-rooted weed such as bindweed. For a week or so, you'll pat yourself on the back. But soon every piece you chopped up will become a new weed. The best control for these sorts of weeds might be to use an herbicide or to smother them with a layer of plastic or newspapers for up to a year. My personal method is to pull them over and over—up to six times—to weaken the plant, then to hit them with an herbicide such as Round-up. My rampaging crop of bindweed appears to be (nearly) extinct, but the tree of heaven that came with

> Whoever said that a weed is just a flower growing in the wrong spot must have been on heavy medication or never ran into the likes of bindweed, kudzu, bittersweet, thistle, and various ivies. 🌹

the place sends out runners as effortlessly as most of us send e-mails. There's even one growing in my laundry room. Yes, in it. I've chopped, dug, and sprayed, but it's a battle of wills. Ordinarily I wouldn't credit a tree with the ability to form intent, but I do wonder when it mounts a home invasion.

When you've conquered the really tough weeds (or if you lucked out and never had to face them at all), the first-year garden still offers challenges. Weeding can take the fun out of the whole experience. It seems never-ending, as weeds of different kinds take their turns and germinate throughout the growing season. Many weed seeds can lie dormant for years or decades, just waiting for an opportunity.

My most persistent of the pesky weeds last season in a new garden area was portulaca. Springing up as thick as dog hair, this fleshy-leafed annual thrives in hot, dry weather, much like its ornamental cousin we usually call moss rose. There was nothing rosy about this picture. Whereas most annuals that I hoe or pluck have the decency to die, portulaca often re-roots. I like to use a tool called an "action" or "shuffle" hoe for annual weeds. It looks a bit like a horseshoe mounted on a handle, with a flat, two-sided blade that cuts just beneath the crust of the soil as you rake it back and forth. It's very useful, but I go back with a rake to pick up the portulaca before it roots again.

I went through about five rounds with the portulaca, cleaning out every last one before a new batch would sprout a week or so later. Cooler temperatures finally turned the tide in my favor, so I expect very little resistance this coming season. The perennials will begin to expand, shading much of the ground, leaving less and less opportunity for portulaca or any other weeds. The third year in a garden for me is generally almost weed-free, leaving more time for the more rewarding chores.

Weeding does have its good points, depending on how efficient you become. There are days I actually enjoy it. Good tools help. A really sturdy dandelion digger is perfect for tap-rooted weeds. Don't buy a cheap one; it won't last a week without bending. I rely heavily on my Japanese fisherman's knife, often called a hori-hori. It can serve for tap-rooted weeds as well as shallow-rooted weeds, because the edge is serrated to cut just below the soil surface. Several kinds of hoes are useful as well, from the previously mentioned hollow type to the standard flat blade or smaller dagger-pointed variety for tight spaces. And some people prefer their bare hands, wrestling victory from the earth in hand-to-hand combat.

Weeding takes up valuable time, so we need to make the most of it. I often play music on headphones. Sometimes I sing. My neighbors frown on this. During the attack of the portulaca, I used the reward system on myself. It goes something like this: "If I get as far as that butterfly bush (or whatever landmark selected), I'll stop for a while, sit in the shade, and possibly find the strength to go inside and find some chocolate." The weeds are gone and I'm still using this system. Now that's a happy ending.

■ Insects, Pests, and Diseases in the Garden

My parents never used insecticides in their garden, so I've grown up pretty ignorant of them. And I intend to keep it that way. People freak out at the sight of the first aphid of the year and overreact with an arsenal of chemical weapons. My advice? Chill. A bug-free garden is as unnatural as one made of artificial flowers. As I've mentioned before, soap is a gardener's best friend. I mix a teaspoon of Dr. Bronner's Castille Oil soap in a spray bottle with a quart of water and have at it. Spraying any pesky aphids I can see (you've got to hit them for the soap to dissolve them), I also make sure to hit the undersides of leaves and stems. This is where most sucking insects like aphids, spider mites, and white flies hang out.

Then there are the chewing insects like caterpillars, beetles, and earwigs. I hate earwigs. It's not that they do any more damage than any other bug; it's just that they're furtive like cockroaches with little pincers in front. I've seen enough science fiction movies to be totally creeped out by the threat they could pose to all humanity.

For every bad bug in the garden, there's one on your side. And along with the ladybugs, lacewings, predatory wasps, praying mantis, and spiders (the good guys) is the bird and bat brigade, which feasts on insects. Start to tinker with this coalition by introducing poisons, and you'll destroy the natural balance. Would you begrudge the caterpillars a meal or two before they transform into butterflies? And no matter how careful you are with chemical sprays and dusts, do you really want to take chances with children, pets, fish, and wildlife?

Of course, there may be critters that you would like to banish from your garden. Depending on where you live, perhaps you'll tangle with mice, squirrels, voles, moles, ground squirrels, gophers, rabbits, skunks, raccoons, deer, elk, or moose—or some combination thereof. Consult your local experts at botanical gardens, nurseries, and extension services on how best to deal with whatever is plaguing you. There are some truly destructive insects and critters out there with which I've never had to deal. Perhaps you may need to at some point. All I can say is that I'd urge you to take the most conservative approach. It never hurts to consult the seasoned gardeners in your neighborhood. Odds are, they've seen it all and may have some clever, environmentally friendly remedies. Approaches work differently in some regions and at certain times of the year.

Some of your staunchest allies are your pets. Both cats and dogs can be deterrents to wildlife, whether they're aggressive protectors or just hanging out on the porch. The mere scent of dogs, for example, puts off deer. I met a man in Montana with a beautiful garden out in the country that wasn't fenced (usually the only reliable way to keep deer out). He'd trained his dog since he was a puppy to mark certain trees and rocks that ringed the property. He and the puppy walked and peed several times a day for several months until it became part of the dog's daily routine.

Still, I'd recommend fencing for best results, since deer will eat the shingles off your house if they're hungry enough. Much is made of deer-resistant plants that they will find unpalatable, as well as soap sprays, hot pepper sprays, blood meal, sirens, flashing lights, and heavy metal music. I'd imagine you'd mostly alarm your neighbors rather than have a lasting effect on a herd of deer with appetites bigger than those of teenagers. I think deer are beautiful creatures when I see them in the mountains, but I can't imagine them grazing in my garden. I think they'd quickly lose their charm. So put up some substantial fencing or get a puppy and go for a stroll.

Plant diseases are no fun. Some are not usually life-threatening, such as mildew, although others such as clematis wilt are fatal. Can you prevent most diseases? Not really. Can you avoid the plants that get them? You bet. Nursing sick plants is grim and depressing. A garden full of mildewed, black-spotted plants is common, but unnecessary. In any region there are hundreds, no thousands, of plants that stay healthy no matter how humid and muggy it gets. Some books will recommend "good air circulation," as if you could place giant fans in pertinent spots in your garden. When plants succumb to disease, they're most likely ill-suited to growing in your region. You can become nursemaid rather than gardener or decide that no matter how lovely a plant might be (somewhere else) you can find a new love. And it's always worth investigating varieties that have natural resistance or have been bred to be resistant.

■ Realistic Maintenance

How much work your garden requires depends on its size, complexity, and the types of plants you grow. It also depends on your temperament. Some of us can easily overlook flaws. Others have this compulsive need to be on top of everything all the time, so we're constantly snipping and clipping. And timing is everything.

When I was five years old, my family moved to a small town on the eastern plains of Colorado. Gardening was a hard-fought battle on that windswept land. My early memories are of flowers, from the lilac and bridal veil bushes that hugged our house, to tulips and tomatoes in the garden, to wild roses and asters in the fields next to our house.

I've gardened for more decades than I care to admit, and it's still a sweaty and dirty business; but I no longer think in terms of war. Fighting nature is an exercise in futility. Accepting soil and weather conditions—and welcoming challenges—yields the most rewards. Knowing what to do—and when—makes gardening a pleasure rather than a chore (depending, of course, on how you feel about sweat and dirt).

Each spring I observe great mistakes. Apartment dwellers imagine their houseplants would appreciate a little sunshine as much as they do and drag them to the balcony; ficus trees and ferns bake to a crisp. Blooming delphiniums and roses fresh from the greenhouse get planted in suburban gardens way too early; a late snowstorm inevitably flattens them like pancakes.

The trickiest time of the gardening season begins in midspring. The key is to balance enthusiasm with caution. Starved for color after our winter abstinence, some of us plant recklessly without consulting the calendar. Each region has a set date considered to be that of the average last frost. In my region, May 15 is the green light to set out warm-season favorites such as tomatoes, peppers, marigolds, and zinnias. But May 15 doesn't come with a guarantee, and it's actually too late for the cool-season annuals such as peas, spinach, leaf lettuce, and pansies. This will likely prove true in your region as well.

In truth, the gardening season begins much earlier than most people think and ends much later as well. Learning what gets planted when—and where—is vitally important. Novice gardeners try to buy tulip bulbs in spring, never guessing that their window of opportunity closed in late fall. Sun-loving roses languish beneath a canopy of trees, while shade-loving hostas fry in a sunny hot spot. Yankees who move down south stick to their old habits and plant their pansies just in time to roast them to a crisp. There's no need. We all make mistakes, and good gardeners learn from them. Just avoid the obvious ones. If you're not killing some plants from time to time, you're not trying very hard to learn how to garden. Experience, of course, is the best teacher. I still kill my fair share of plants; it's just more embarrassing for me.

Perhaps we should talk a bit about shopping before we talk about the art of planting and the other garden skills. Shopping is one of my favorite parts of gardening. You say you're good at it? You'll make a great gardener. Shop in stores throughout the season and from winter catalogs

Imagine the pleasure of tending this productive plot devoted to squash and corn, as well as to flowers for cutting—cosmos, marigolds, and sunflowers.

and your garden will never be dull. I rarely see crummy, poorly grown plants at a nursery these days, so I'm not going to go into a long spiel about selecting healthy plants. Look for good foliage color and you might check beneath the leaves for bugs—but I don't do that, so why should you? There will probably be a few roots poking out from the drainage holes in the bottom of the plant's pot. That's fine. If they're longer than a few inches and the root ball is threatening to bust out, the plant is known as "pot bound." This hasn't ever stopped me from buying a plant. You simply take it home, cut it out of its plastic prison, and try to trim and help separate the roots a bit. Then give it a loving home in the ground or a new pot.

■ Basic Skills

There are a few basic skills to learn to become a good gardener. They're all easily mastered. Most become second nature in time. Intuition plays a big part in figuring out what to do and

Whoever writes nursey tags for plants lives in a Camelot of gardening where plants reach amazing proportions never seen elsewhere.

when. Avoid making work for yourself. If everything looks all right, let sleeping dogs lie. Don't go out and hack at your bushes just because you think you should be doing something.

PLANTING

Planting is the most important skill you can learn. Do it gently, but firmly. The best way to learn is to watch an experienced gardener at work. Go to a botanical garden if there's one nearby to observe. Better yet, volunteer so you can get hands-on experience.

To plant your newly purchased plants, dig a hole larger than the pots in which they came. Turn the pots upside down with one hand, holding the other hand underneath to catch them, and coax the plants out gently (gravity will do most of the work); no yanking and pulling out by the stems. Plant them at the same level that they're growing in their pots, but in a slight depression. Gently pack the soil around the plant, but no stomping. Just use the strength in your hands.

As you work, build a little mud wall about 2" high around each plant to capture moisture. "Puddle in" each plant with a very slow trickle of the hose until it's thoroughly saturated. Each plant is essentially still in its container, so water deeply each time, probably every four to seven days for a gallon-size perennial, depending on your soil and weather. If you live in a cold winter area, fertilize every couple of weeks through July, and then stop so the plants can begin to prepare for cooler fall weather. In their second year, perennials need little or no fertilizer.

TRANSPLANTING

There comes a time when you'll want to divide and transplant a perennial. This is best done in early spring just as the plant emerges, but hardly anybody gets around to it then. You can basically do it any time except during the real summer heat. Dig it up (a digging fork is easiest, but a shovel will do). Cut it in half or in several pieces depending on its size. The blade of a spade works well. Give it a hard thrust. You can also use a sturdy kitchen knife.

Transplanting is just like planting, except that you usually give your subject a haircut before you replant. This generally means cutting back the top growth so the roots don't have so much to support while they're reestablishing themselves. The plant should end up at the same level it was growing at before you started. Again, create an earthen dam around the base to catch and hold water and thoroughly soak the soil immediately after planting.

GROWING FROM SEED

Sowing seeds is much less work than planting. Some kinds can be simply sprinkled over the soil as if you were feeding chickens. I usually do this in either fall or late winter with annuals such as larkspurs, poppies, and bachelor's buttons. Vegetable seeds are usually but not always planted in rows, at the appropriate time for each kind. After digging and leveling the site with a rake, use a hoe to create a furrow 1" or so deep. Then plant the corn, peas, beans, or whatever you like, covering the seeds about a ¼" to ½" deep. Space the seeds a few inches apart, knowing that as they germinate and grow, you'll need to thin them to allow room for each one to develop. How much to thin depends on what you're growing. Radishes need only a few inches in between, while corn needs a foot.

Sowing seeds inside is a bit easier, mainly because you're sitting down. The easiest way for most of us is to fill plastic six-pack plant containers with a soil mixture especially formulated for seedlings. Plant a few seeds per cell (you'll need to thin later), covering them as directed on the seed packet. Water from the bottom by soaking the containers in their trays or you'll probably wash the seeds all over the place. Seed packets also tell you when to plant, generally four to eight weeks before the average frost-free date in your area, so count backward from that date. It helps to get this all organized on paper in midwinter, plus it gives us something to dream about when winter seems never-ending.

SPACING PLANTS

How much room your plants need between them is very tricky. I pay attention to the growth estimates for trees and shrubs and space accordingly. For perennials and annuals, I tend to follow my own instincts because I don't trust the nursery tags. Whoever writes them lives in a far-off Camelot land of gardening where plants reach amazing proportions never seen elsewhere. So for where I live in the mountain West, I cut the recommended spacing down by at least a third and sometimes by half. My theory is that most of us prefer results during our lifetimes.

Glorious dahlias result from pinching, staking, fertilizing, and deadheading. They're worth the fuss.

FEEDING PLANTS

Once everything is planted and growing, feed your plants. There's no set standard; some plants are heavier feeders than others. Some don't want or need any supplemental fertilization at all. Just as a general guideline, be generous with roses, bulbs, most annuals, containerized plants, and vegetables. Most trees, shrubs, vines, herbs, and perennials can get along pretty well on their own. Many people overfeed their perennials and end up with a bunch of lax, floppy plants. Then they have to stake them. I don't like staking and I rarely grow plants that are bred to fall over, but occasionally I make an exception. You probably will, too.

PLANT SUPPORTS

My weakness is dahlias. The tall ones need stakes. I grow them in pots on my patio for their huge, eye-popping blossoms in the heat of summer and into fall. I pinch my dahlias when they're about 6" tall. This means I tweak out the growing tip with my thumb and forefinger. This causes them to branch out and get bushy. Pinching is great to help avoid tall thin plants. Try it on petunias, flowering tobacco, pansies, flowering maples, and geraniums to get really floriferous plants. But back to stakes. When necessary—and before your lanky plant blows over— insert at the base a sturdy bamboo pole as tall as the plant is projected to reach. Use yarn, string, or twist-ties every 10", attaching it first to the stake and then around the plant stem. Sometimes I use tree branches with a "Y" joint (like one you'd use to make a sling-shot) and simply prop up a droopy plant. This kind of staking is barely noticeable. You can also buy metal supports and hoops. These are useful for top-heavy flowers such as peonies, which too often display their blossoms in the mud.

DEADHEADING, SHAPING, AND PRUNING

Most plants need grooming. The most common cleanup is deadheading, which has nothing to do with concerts. It's simply cutting or pinching off faded blossoms and their stems. The technique varies. For a Shasta daisy, for example, take off the flower and its long stem where it emerges from the base of leaves. For a begonia, just pinch off the spent flower. Deadheading encourages plants to keep blooming rather than putting their energies into seed production. Sometimes the entire plant is cut back to persuade it to regenerate and re-bloom. These summer cutbacks are for June bloomers that look tired and worn out in July. Now's your chance to do some serious whacking, cutting back many perennials by half or more—sometimes all the way to the ground. A list of candidates that prosper after a cutback (and a subsequent feeding) include many daisies, meadow sage, lupine, columbine, and catmint.

You can always do a bit of shaping and pruning when you like, but most people do too much. For most of us, early spring is the best time to cut out dead branches on trees and shrubs and do minimal shaping. This is also the time to cut back perennials and ornamental grasses. Meadows can simply be mowed. The old idea that the garden needs to be put to bed in fall has pretty much gone by the wayside. Save your autumnal energy for planting bulbs and moving pots of tropical plants inside. Nowadays we leave perennials, grasses, and even some annuals alone as winter comes, the better to enjoy their freeze-dried beauty. This also helps to protect the crowns of the plants from the extremes of winter.

■ Tips to Save Energy: Yours and the Garden's

The rhythm of a garden isn't a constant one. Nor is a gardener's. In spring most of us have energy to burn. That's good because there's plenty to be accomplished. Last year's perennials and grasses are cut back in mid- to late winter, depending on where you live. At about the same time, cool-season annuals and vegetables need to be sown outdoors. Peas, for example, are traditionally planted on St. Patrick's Day across the northern tier of states. In the meantime, many gardeners get a jump on the growing season by starting warm-season annuals and vegetables indoors.

The weather plays us like a yo-yo. It's too cold. Then it's warming up. No, wait—it's still too cold. Well, it feels pretty mild; maybe I should start transplanting and spading the vegetable patch. Oops, it's snowing. The moisture was good anyway. Now maybe it's okay. It was still pretty chilly last night. It's been 90 degrees for a week now. Oh dear, is it too late to plant tomatoes? This weather roller coaster can really wear you down. In the beginning of the season (spring, that is) we all invariably overdo it. We're not yet garden tough, so sore muscles and strained backs become common. Our bodies tone and strengthen as the season progresses. By mid-June, we're feeling pretty buff.

> **In the beginning of the season (spring, that is) we all invariably overdo it. We're not yet garden tough.**

Then it hits. The heat, humidity, grasshoppers, and crabgrass start to take their toll. We've reached the summer energy crisis. In what's supposed to be the time when we most enjoy our gardens, we can become too worn out. It seems only the super-gardener can shrug off the summer's setbacks to keep his or her garden picture-perfect. I'm no super-gardener, but my midsummer garden looks pretty cool. Here's how:

- Water plants in early morning, deeply and only when necessary (remember, poke your fingers into the soil to see how much moisture your plants have).
- Count on container plantings for color and substance (these are the plants you can most easily control); use tropicals and other heat lovers.
- Give your plants plenty of food and water (especially for the container plantings); install drip lines in the garden if you're mechanically inclined.
- Cut back early-blooming perennials.
- Select a different, small area to be groomed each day. Give it 20 minutes or whatever time you can. Move on to a new area the next day.
- Wear light-colored clothing along with broad-brimmed hats when you garden.
- Don't sweat the small stuff, such as deadheading. There's always next week.
- The best time to pull a weed is when you see it.

■ Essential Garden Tools

What tools do you need? Forgive me if I say, "It depends." There are some perfectly nice tools I've never used, so I can only tell you what I find "essential" and "nice to have." Let's start with the ones I use most. The Japanese fisherman's knife, called a hori-hori, features a 7" steel blade, serrated on one side, with a wood or plastic handle. Its primary uses include weeding, planting small stuff, and, presumably, gutting fish. A hori-hori costs about $20 to $35 depending on the model you get. Only one major caveat: Keep this tool out of reach of your children!

PRUNERS AND LOPPERS

The next essential is a pair of pruners, also called secauters by people who don't think pruners is descriptive enough. There are several different styles. I'd suggest a basic pair with a grip that feels comfortable. You'll get plenty of use out of a pair of pruners when you cut back the garden in spring, prune shrubs and small tree branches, deadhead flowers, and harvest herbs. I'd splurge and get a good pair (meaning, lifetime), for which you'll spend close to $50. Loppers are like bigger pruners and can handle slightly larger limbs up to about 1 ½" in diameter. They're nice to have around (I borrow my neighbors'). You can get a decent lopper for about $30.

DIGGING TOOLS

Still in the essentials, you need a spade or shovel (unless you're a rooftop gardener and never dig in the earth). The classic shovel is for digging. Buy a good quality one that won't break when you do something dumb like pry a boulder out with it. Of course, now you say you wouldn't do anything like that—but you will. You can buy a decent shovel at the hardware store for $15 and up. A rubber coating at the end of the handle may help prevent blisters. A spade has a flat spade. I like my "border" spade a lot. It cost about $50, and I'll probably have it forever. I mainly use it for dividing: once you've dug up a big clump of daylilies or whatever, a good thrust with the blade will cut it cleanly in half. For people of petite stature, try a lady's spade, which is a smaller version, or a border spade, which is pretty much the same thing. I like this tool for working in tight quarters to dig holes for bulbs or new perennials.

I also get good use from my digging fork. It looks a bit like a pitchfork, but has longer, thinner tines and is much lighter. A digging fork is a sturdy tool, usually with four or five steel tines that are designed to loosen a vegetable garden's soil before planting or to lift clumps of perennials for transplanting or dividing. A cheap version of this tool will bend when confronted by heavy, wet soil, hidden rocks or debris, or a really entrenched shrub rose that you've decided to move. So do invest in a better tool that will stand the test of time.

Since we're still discussing digging tools, I'd also spring for a good-quality trowel. Essentially a miniature, hand-held spade, a trowel is designed for digging small holes for things like perennials and annuals. A good strong handle and sturdy blade are necessary. You'll bend a cheap one in two days. The point of contention is where the handle meets the blade. If this isn't securely joined, it will fall apart. One-piece forged pieces of stainless steel get around this problem. Be prepared to pay at least $25 for a good trowel.

I occasionally use my dibble, which is a quaint tool for making uniform holes for seeds or small bulbs. It's essentially a pointed, plump piece of wood (like a swollen wooden carrot) that you can probably live without. But it does look picturesque on the potting bench. Speaking of which, do you need a proper potting bench? I admire the really nice ones immensely, with their stainless-steel tops and compartments for potting soil and stuff. I usually do my seeding on the dining table or kitchen floor and I plant my containers in place on the patio or balcony. Still, a potting bench would look really stylish in my sunroom.

RAKES

Most people rake more than I do; I lack the obsession to remove every leaf and blade of grass that falls. When I had a lawn, I used a mulching mower (which I highly recommend) to chop up the leaves in my last fall mowing. I leave most leaves where they fall in the garden itself to protect plants and disintegrate over the winter. This is a judgment call, because too many leaves can compact into a slimy mess that smothers rather than protects your plants. But

Even when its days of service are over, a leaky wheelbarrow positioned by the tool shed holds a bevy of beautiful daylilies, liatris, and 'Moonbeam' coreopsis.

to the subject of rakes: a lightweight, aluminum leaf rake is pretty much indispensable around your property (you can get back-saving ergonomic models, as you can with many kinds of tools as well as those for lefties). Even better for working among plants in fall or spring is a rake with rubber tines that won't tear up your perennials. A small hand rake really comes in handy for tight spots.

A heavy iron garden rake gets most of its use in the vegetable garden for leveling and smoothing after digging. I often turn the head upside down to get rid of dirt clods by beating them with it. I'm not kidding; it's the best way.

HOES

Not everyone needs a hoe. I use a standard type, mainly for making furrows for planting seeds of corn, beans, and other vegetables. I used to have an old hoe that must have been in the garage when I bought the house. Poorly designed and constructed, the blade would occasionally fly off the handle. I was doing some serious weeding one day, chopping out clumps of grass and clover, when the flying-off-the-handle episodes became more frequent and dangerous.

Few things in gardening cause as much cussing as a hose that kinks.

So get a quality hoe that will stay in one piece. Another hoe I use more frequently is the "action" or "shuffle" hoe, which has a thin sharp blade on a hollow head that shuffles back and forth, and which cuts small weeds off just below the soil surface.

HOSES AND GARDEN MISCELLANY

Even if you put in an automated underground irrigation system, you'll still need a hose. Few things in gardening cause as much cussing as a hose that kinks. You'll pay more for a quality hose, but, again, you'll keep your cool. Get one longer than you think you'll need. A 50' hose is shorter than you imagined.

Among the things I use on a constant basis are plastic spray bottles (for soap sprays), a plastic ten-gallon bucket for toting tools and collecting garden debris, a hose reel for quick roll-ups, and various hose attachments. For container gardening, I use a watering wand with an adjustable head that I can dial up to get everything from a fine mist to a powerful jet. It's similar to the one you may have in your shower that pulses and massages. The advantage is that you can get a delicate spray so that you don't wash away seedlings, or a more aggressive spray for washing down the patio and everything in between.

Among the tools I've yet to find a use for are the hand claw (I don't think my plants would want me disturbing their roots on a daily basis) and the bulb planter, an aluminum tube that would be better for taking geological core samples if it weren't guaranteed to bring on carpal tunnel syndrome within three minutes of use. Surely I've had a few others that have long been buried in the back corners of the potting shed.

Once your relatives and friends see that you've become a gardener, you're bound to get garden stuff as gifts. If they garden, perhaps they'll give you useful things like pots and tools. Try to steer them in the right direction so that they don't give you trinkets like pink flamingos and resin plaques that say "My Garden" or "Squirrel Crossing."

■ Start to Plant!

At some point you'll need to stop reading, quit planning, and go buy some plants. Get yourself to your local nursery. Ask for help. Try not to get distracted by every pretty flower you see. Follow your list just like at the grocery store. There are plenty of suggestions within the regional section of this book, which immediately follows this introduction.

Part of being a good gardener is being a good observer. Watch what happens in your garden through the seasons and learn from it. As your thumb starts to get a little green glow, branch out and try new things. If you do indeed kill a plant (and you will), figure out why. Plants want to live, so something went wrong. The answer is usually that the plant received too much or too little water. Always poke your finger in the soil several inches deep before you water. If it's moist, hold off.

You're off and running. Take some classes. Read some more books. Get dirty.

🌸 Section 2

Your Southwest Garden

his guide is designed to meet the needs of new gardeners in Arizona, New Mexico, Nevada, southern Utah, and southwestern Colorado. The region includes U.S. Department of Agriculture (USDA) climate zones 4 to 11. (Look on the climate zone map in the front of the book to locate your zone.) The USDA climate zones are based on the average minimum temperature at which plants can survive for each area. It is especially important to pay attention to these zones when planting trees, shrubs, and long-lived perennials, although you can usually fudge a little on annuals and short-lived perennials.

The first step on the journey toward a beautiful southwestern garden is to embrace your natural surroundings. Get to know your territory. Next, figure out how you will work with its attributes for the best possible garden for the place in which you live. Instead of bemoaning the

---

Drifts of colorful, long-blooming perennials, a native piñon pine, and ground cover of silver-leaved snow-in-summer combine in an informal southwestern entry garden.

arid southwestern conditions and investing labor and materials to change them, wise gardeners try to take advantage of conditions wherever and whenever possible and only try to modify them within reason. Whether you call this approach climate-wise gardening, natural gardening, or ecological gardening, it makes sense and it works!

After reading the book's overall introduction, you probably understand basic gardening ideas and terminology pretty well—and whether or not you're feeling entirely confident, I'll bet you can hold your own in any gardening conversation. This is sure to come in handy soon as you venture out into the world to select tools, seeds, plants, and hardscape items (remember the term "hardscape"—it means all of the nonliving features that serve as a framework to hold your garden together and show off plants to their best advantage). Give yourself a pat on the back before we move on. What you learned from the first section of this book would take up nearly an entire semester's course in horticulture (the art and science of growing plants)—and it's the greater part of what you'll need to get started with your southwestern garden. The rest of what you need to know will come from taking stock of where you are, from the experience you gain as you work on your own garden, and from the give-and-take of sharing information with others who garden in your community.

A nongardening friend of mine tells me she's afraid to go into local nurseries because she feels she's under scrutiny as a novice. Don't let your newness at gardening make you feel that way—almost every plant lover likes to share, so go ahead and ask questions! Soon enough you'll be surprised to find yourself the experienced gardener sharing your own firsthand knowledge with others.

Like Rob Proctor, the author of this book's introduction, I grew up in a neighborhood of gardeners. Everyone got in on the act and grew something. This kind of upbringing is common among plant people. But if you're just starting out on your first garden, chances are you weren't raised on gardening—or if you were, it was in a very different environment. Don't worry about it. The good thing about being a grown-up is that you can catch up on things very quickly! You'll learn by osmosis, imitation, and playful personal experience. So think of me as your guide to the Southwest, a good neighbor who'll share some hard-earned gardening wisdom. Then keep your eyes open for local guides in your immediate area—the woman down the street who tends the extravagant bougainvillea; the man around the corner with the most gracefully shaped mesquite trees; or the person at the garden center who always takes care of the customers who ask tough questions. They'll be the ones who help you practice what you're learning and help make your garden wish list into a living, growing garden.

■ Setting the Stage for Your Southwest Garden

To get started in the Southwest, you'll need to give some thought to all of the characteristics that make this region special. The southwestern landscape is influenced by Native American, Hispanic, and pioneer heritages. While we live in the presence of ancient cultures, many things are new here. The landscape is dotted with small rural settlements of fiercely independent farmers and ranchers, land-based tribal people, and burgeoning urban areas that still have strong ties to the natural landscape. Water is scarce and precious throughout the region, which has vast and varied topography (elevations ranging from just below sea level to over 12,000'). Plants in the

With creamy yellow and green strap-shaped succulent leaves and striking form, this variegated American agave is a noteworthy garden focal point.

Southwest, from low desert scrub to dense evergreen spruce-fir forests, require special adaptations to survive extremes of heat, cold, and drought. All of this makes for interesting gardens.

Whenever I read gardening books that say the Southwest has a horrible climate—monstrous heat, blinding sunlight, poor soils, and inadequate rainfall—I think back to the cheery, daisy-covered poster in my sixth grade classroom. It said "Bloom where you are planted!" Those English daisies on that poster? They would have trouble here in the Southwest. Our southwestern posters tend to feature a stately saguaro cactus, a quaking aspen, or a striking red penstemon being visited by a darting hummingbird. In the right southwestern garden, each of these plants will bloom where it is planted with the addition of just a little water to get it going and a little care to keep it looking its best. If we try the English daisy (*Bellis perennis*) here, it will only thrive if we give it shade, acidify the soil, fertilize regularly, and provide nearly constant water. Forget to water for a week and it's gone, period!

Once you've created your first successful southwestern garden, you'll look at all gardens a little differently—judging them not on lush greenness and dazzling bloom, but rather on the form, color, texture, fragrance, and compatibility with their surroundings of their plantings.

In this section, we'll talk about regional characteristics and how working with these will ease your gardening tasks. We'll talk about ways savvy southwestern gardeners meet their unique

**Fragrant Mexican evening primrose flowers look delicate,
but these natives are one of the best low-maintenance ground covers for dry slopes.**

gardening challenges. We'll showcase 50 beautiful easy-to-grow plants that are proven to do well in southwestern gardens. And later we've provided the resource section to help you find inspiration, local information, plants, and services to help you make your garden a success.

KNOW WHERE YOU ARE

Since you're living in the Southwest, or are planning on joining us soon, chances are you already know there are big differences in the way our gardens look and feel compared with ones you've seen in other parts of the country. On television, most Americans are multimillionaires, and, no matter where they live, their gardens come straight out of *Beverly Hills 90210*. Beside every swimming pool are palm trees, hibiscus, giant tree ferns, ever-blooming geraniums, and a host of plants so water-loving and tender most would fade out in a day in our demanding southwestern climate. Then there are the home improvement shows. Garden redos abound. But most of these gardens are in the humid climes of Hawaii, Florida, or Massachusetts—or even farther away in the sunny south of France or balmy old England. Enjoy the shows—but realize that in the Southwest the only place where you can create that kind of a lush green paradise is in an enclosed dome with more water than most people can afford to buy.

For more than 200 years, eastern ideals of garden beauty set the standard in this country. Southwestern gardeners long tried to mimic northeastern gardens by filling our gardens with plants that make about as much sense in our climate as New England boiled dinner on a salsa bar. But times have changed! New schools of gardening celebrate each unique region with native and adapted plants, local materials, and regional culture. Gardens do well when they are in tune with the natural world rather than fighting it tooth and nail every step of the way. New gardens

WHICH NATIVE PLANTS ARE RIGHT FOR YOU? TYPICAL NATIVE PLANTS FOR SOUTHWESTERN GARDENS

HABITAT	ELEVATION	RAINFALL	REPRESENTATIVE LOCATIONS	TYPICAL NATIVE PLANTS
Subalpine mixed coniferous forest	8,000' to 12,400'	>24"	highest mountains	aspen, bristlecone pine, gooseberry, kinnikinnick, mountain muhly grass, scarlet carpet bugler
Ponderosa pine forest	5,500' to 10,000'	20" to 24"	Flagstaff, AZ; Chama, NM	blue grama grass, creeping barberry, Englemann prickly pear cactus, Gambel oak, golden currant, sulfur buckwheat, white fir
Piñon–juniper woodland	3,400' to 8,900'	15" to 19"	Sedona, AZ; Trinidad, CO; Santa Fe, NM	banana yucca, Eaton's firecracker, little bluestem grass, juniper, piñon pine, sagebrush, three-leaf sumac, wine cup
Evergreen-oak woodland	3,900' to 5,300'	20" to 24"	Oracle, AZ	Arizona white oak, beargrass, desert spoon, Indian pink, little bluestem grass, silk tassel bush
Great Basin montane scrub	7,000' to 9,000'	16" to 20"	Durango, CO; Bryce Canyon, UT	big-tooth maple, chamisa, Gambel oak, lupine, mountain mahogany, snowberry, wild rose
Interior chaparral	3,300' to 6,600'	16" to 20"	Miami, AZ; Cureton, NM	Arizona cypress, goldenaster, live oak, manzanita, Palmer's penstemon, Parry's agave, sideoats grama grass
Plains and Great Basin prairies	3,900' to 7,600'	8" to 10"	Winslow, AZ; Southern Colorado; Albuquerque, NM	evening primrose, four o'clock, Indian grass, prickly pear cactus, sand sage, sideoats grama grass, soapweed yucca
Semidesert grassland	3,300' to 6,200'	10" to 12"	Kingman, AZ; Lordsburg, NM	desert spoon, golden-flowered agave, juniper, mesquite, soaptree yucca, tobosa
Great Basin desert scrub	3,900' to 8,500'	7" to 12"	Page, AZ; Cortez, CO; Taos, NM; Bluff, UT	chamisa, Indian ricegrass, juniper, plains prickly pear, sagebrush, wild buckwheat, Utah agave
Mojave desert scrub	2,900' to 3,900'	4" to 9"	Las Vegas, NV; St. George, UT	desert needlegrass, desert senna, globe mallow, Joshua tree, Mormon tea, silver cholla, Spanish dagger
Chihuahuan desert scrub	3,100' to 4,600'	10" to 14"	Tombstone, AZ; Carlsbad, NM	creosote, desert spoon, desert sumac, guajillo, mariola, prairie zinnia, tobosa
Lower Colorado River Sonoran desert scrub	200' to 1,500'	3" to 8"	Parker, Phoenix, and Yuma, AZ	brittlebush, chuparosa, desert honeysuckle, desert lavender, desert willow, honey mesquite, jojoba
Upland Sonoran stem succulent desert	900' to 3,000'	8" to 13"	Ajo, Carefree, and Tucson, AZ	desert prickly pear, fairy duster, little-leaf palo verde, mesquite, night-blooming cactus, ocotillo, organ pipe cactus, saguaro cactus, teddy bear cholla
Riparian woodland	all elevations	varies	along rivers and streams	big-tooth maple, blue spruce, canyon grape, cottonwood, elderberry, velvet ash, willows, yellow monkeyflower

are utilitarian, too! Today, a southwestern garden that doesn't include at least a few edible plants and herbs is passé.

Nearly all southwestern gardens experience brilliant sunlight, strong winds, a dry spring season, wide temperature swings (sometimes as much as 40 to 50 degrees Fahrenheit in a single day), mineral soils, limited rainfall, high evaporation rate, low humidity, extreme heat and cold, late and early frosts, grasshoppers, and enough wild critters to populate *Animal Planet*. Sure, there are a few moist areas with rich soils. If you live on the banks of a stream or river, count yourself lucky! But for the most part, southwestern conditions are far more demanding—and rewarding.

To meet our challenges, southwestern gardeners have developed special approaches and techniques that work here. You'll never get bored with an endless sea of green, since our gardens are as varied as our natural surroundings, filled with colorful regional delights like cacti, chiles, citrus, apples, pears, penstemons, peaches, cilantro, bird-of-paradise bushes, ocotillos, banana yuccas, coneflowers, agaves, piñon pines, palo verdes, creosotes, and quaking aspens. Guiding your plant selection and governing the timing of your gardening activities are elevation, date of first and last frost, timing and amount of rain and snow, water quality, sun and shade, micro-climates, nearby native vegetation type, and degree of fire hazard.

In the Southwest, temperature and rainfall change rapidly with elevation, topography, and aspect (the direction a slope faces). In low deserts, summer days are very hot. Even plants need a midday siesta. High elevations have days and nights too cool for year-round gardening. As a rule, as elevations rise, temperatures go down and precipitation increases.

But local weather conditions can be just that—local. I live in the mountains of northern Arizona. Some days I stand at the kitchen sink and look out the front window to a calm untroubled day. When I turn my head and look out the back door, whistling winds are filling the air with dust and blowing our laundry horizontal on the clothesline. My front yard is usually 10 degrees warmer and has a growing season that is 15 days longer than in my back yard. If I want to see my New Mexico sunflowers bloom, I have to put them in the front yard; otherwise it will never happen. Do you remember the "microclimates" mentioned in the first section? What I just described is a very good example.

Whenever I think about seasons, I hear a little child's voice in my mind repeating "spring showers bring summer flowers." You get the picture, right? For southwestern gardeners, that progression of seasons and how it relates to plant growth needs a bit of tweaking. To begin with, April, May, and June are the three months of the year when we are least likely to have any significant rainfall. Spring can be cold, spring can be hot, spring can be sunny, and spring is almost certainly windy—but no showers!

GROWING SEASONS—WHEN TO PLANT

Rainfall patterns, combined with temperatures, determine the planting season for your area. The best times to plant are when moisture is available and daytime temperatures are warm, but not extremely hot. In most of the Southwest, moisture comes during two seasons: winter rains (or snows at high elevations) and tropical summer rainstorms called monsoons. In low-elevation deserts (e.g., Yuma and the cold Mojave desert near Las Vegas, Nevada, along with the adjacent portion of Arizona), precipitation is sparse and occurs only in winter. In hot deserts and mid-elevations, the intense heat of summer signals the end of the growing season and triggers summer

**LEFT: 'Moonshine' yarrow and sunrose thrive with infrequent watering and bright sunlight.
RIGHT: Fall is the best time of year to plant many flowering perennials, including these tall hollyhocks.**

dormancy in many plants. At high elevations, plants stop growing (and often shed leaves or die back to the ground) when soil temperatures begin to stay below freezing.

If you live in Las Vegas or Henderson, Nevada, or Lake Havasu, Arizona, just remember instead "winter showers bring spring flowers." Plant perennials and cool-season vegetables in fall to early winter, take a break until the last spring frost, then plant warm-season vegetables. Savvy gardeners in this dry region will seize the opportunity to plant whenever nighttime temperatures are above freezing, and continue planting until daytime highs are just too hot!

Your own optimal growing season is the time when conditions are best for plant growth. In cold mountain areas, this period typically begins in late May and continues throughout October. As elevation decreases, the growing season begins earlier in spring and continues later into the autumn. At intermediate elevations (3,000–5,000'), both heat and cold can limit the growing season. At the lowest elevations (below 2000'), most plants—with the exception of cool-season vegetables—will grow in all but the hottest months, and a few plants thrive on heat year round.

Planting—From High to Low

To recap, we'll start in the lowlands, then climb. In the warmest, low-desert regions (USDA zones 10 and 11), winter lows rarely, if ever, dip down to freezing. Most rain falls in winter—and if you live in Yuma, Phoenix, or another low-desert community, that is the best time to plant perennials, wildflower seed, and cool-season vegetables in your garden. (If you can't restrain yourself from planting until your winter season, you can start in October, but you'll have to water quite a bit to keep new plants alive until rain arrives.) In your spring season, you can continue planting perennials and warm-season vegetables until scorching days set in—which may be as early as March. If water is available, warm-season vegetables will continue to thrive for a while longer. Sooner or later, summer becomes so hot you won't even want to set foot outdoors during daylight hours—only a few heat-loving plants like red bird-of-paradise look their best at this time of year.

A little higher in the desert (say, Tucson), you can start planting a little sooner when things start to cool down (September through March). Winter nights get colder, with an occasional freeze. Perennials can be planted anytime except the hottest months. Vegetables are planted when soils are warm (September through October for cool-season vegetables, April through June for warm-season vegetables). In Albuquerque, New Mexico, and other mid-elevation areas, plant perennials, wildflower seed, and cool-season vegetables from fall to early spring, and warm-season vegetables once soils are warm. Gardeners in Santa Fe, southern Utah, and southwestern Colorado can plant in fall, take the winter off, and plant again in spring.

In high-elevation mountain towns like Flagstaff, Arizona, or Chama, New Mexico, hailstorms and even late snows are common in May and the last hard frost usually hits in mid-June. Despite spring weather that can include late frosts, cold nights, and sunny, windy, and very dry days, we often put out our annuals once or twice before we should have—only to watch them be hammered by hail or frozen to black mush. Onions, sugar peas, and other cool-season vegetables can be put out in May. Perennial plants may green up in May. But no matter how much you may water, nothing starts to grow until the summer monsoons come (usually around July 4). Gardens flourish until the first killing frost knocks out warm-season vegetables.

In nearly every southwestern climate zone, fall is the best time to plant perennials. The season's shorter, cooler days allow new plantings to establish quickly and easily.

In the desert, sow wildflower seeds in fall to winter. At high elevations, wildflowers that need a winter chill should be seeded in fall. Yet other seeds do well when seed is scattered at the beginning of summer monsoons. (Always rake seeds in lightly after you broadcast them.) Wherever and whenever you plant wildflowers, they will need a period of continuous moisture to establish themselves. If nature does not oblige you, be ready to turn on a sprinkler or use a hose.

Frost-free Days

The number of frost-free days in the Southwest ranges from fewer than 90 days in the coldest area (zone 4) to as many as 350 days in the hottest desert area (zone 11). In cold winter areas, "season extenders" can lengthen the growing season. These extenders can be as elaborate as heated greenhouses or as simple as cold frames (unheated outdoor hardscape structures). With the aid of cold frames, closed at night to protect plants from cold air and opened in daylight hours to keep plants from overheating, you can grow cool-season crops all winter long in cold areas and start warm-season crops early. (Fit cold frames with automatic openers since sooner or later you *will* forget to open or close them.)

Walls of water are water-filled vinyl ministructures, available in nurseries and home improvement stores, that provide protection from winds and late frosts so that gardeners can get an early start on planting tender warm-season vegetables. Squashes, melons, pumpkins, and cucumbers need hot soils to grow vigorously and bear fruit. In all but the hottest areas, a cover of black

Planted near a rock-rimmed pond, purple coneflowers, which thrive in alkaline soils, create a haven where birds, bees, and butterflies can drink, sun, and sup.

plastic mulch will heat soils for warm-season vegetable crops. You will need to place a soaker hose under the black plastic in order to water these plants.

■ Standing Your Ground: Amending, Mulching, and Fertilizing

As mentioned in the introductory section, most soils in the Southwest have neutral to alkaline pH. That's exactly what southwestern garden plants grow best in! Soil characteristics reflect those of their parent materials. Soils of volcanic origin are frequently heavy clays or coarse cinders; sandstone weathers to form sands; and limestone becomes coarse-textured, well-draining soil. Adobes are heavy clays with very fine particles and are sticky when wet. Sandy soil can be pure sand, or in White Sands, New Mexico, made of gypsum, which resembles white snow.

To garden, you don't have to know the exact proportions of your soil components. But knowing this helps you understand better how your soil behaves. To learn more about your soil, simply dig a trowelful, place it in a jar of water with a top, shake it until dispersed, and let it sit until it settles into layers. Organic matter forms the shallow top layer. Beneath this you will find fine-textured clay, mid-sized silt, and a bottom layer of coarse-textured sand. Soils with more than 40 percent clay particles are clays. They hold a lot of water, get sticky, and drain slowly. Soils with at least 70 percent sand particles are sands. They drain rapidly. More equal proportions of sand and clay lead to soils with intermediate water-holding capacity and properties.

A dry wash lined with rounded river rock channels runoff to the roots of this broad-crowned pomegranate tree, creating a mini-oasis with lush growth and delicious fruit.

In desert areas, you may encounter a hardpan or caliche rock layer somewhere beneath the soil surface. This layer limits the flow of water and can therefore hold water like a bathtub, which is not available to your plants. If you are going to plant trees and deep-rooted plants on hardpan, you will need to break through it to create drainage. Amending soils with gypsum helps break down caliche. Soil pores hold air and transport water. Compacted soils greatly inhibit plant growth. To limit compaction, avoid walking or moving equipment on soils when they are wet. You can loosen compacted soils by digging with a garden fork and adding organic matter to keep them open.

SOIL AMENDMENTS

The success and beauty of a garden depend not just on plants, but on all the organic and inorganic materials that are used in the planting, construction, and ornamentation of the garden. Organic matter is once-living material. Some organic matter, like driftwood, cactus skeletons, or fallen wood, can be a decorative element in the garden because it adds form or texture, serves as a focal point, or contributes a sense of place. Most organic matter, however, is used for mulching or for amending soil.

Soil amendments are materials dug into soil to open it up, improve its structure, and increase its water-holding capacity, oxygen level, and fertility. They support the beneficial microorganisms that build soils and help plants grow. Soils in the Southwest are always low in organic matter. Digging some in can help keep clays open and help sands hold water. Composted organic matter and composted manure are two commonly available soil amendments. A word of warning—avoid amending soils with peat moss in the Southwest—once dry, it is virtually impossible to remoisten.

Working with locally available materials can reduce your gardening costs. Also, recycling organic "waste" reduces the size of our landfills. Depending on where you live, organic materials such as tree trimmings, grass, compost, pine needles, sawdust, wood shavings, straw, wood chips, and manure are available, often for free. Stables, poultry farms, and ranches can also be good sources of organic materials. In my community, neighbors rake up pine needles and place them along curbs for pickup; others with deciduous trees bag leaves and put them out curbside. Most folks would be happy for a knock on the door and an offer to rake and take away leaves or needles.

I love composting—the process of taking waste and making it into black gold makes me feel like a real magician! If you haven't tried making your own compost, this is a good time to get started. Set aside a convenient area, and layer materials high in carbon (sawdust, dry leaves, egg shells, nut shells, cornhusks and cobs, citrus peels, coffee grounds) with materials high in nitrogen (most kitchen scraps, weeds, grass clippings, hair, fur, and manure). You may want to place a wire fence or compost bin around your pile to contain it. Adding soil or commercial compost starters helps the process. Compost should be moist, but not wet. Turn compost frequently with a pitchfork. Compost should never smell bad—if it does, turn it more frequently. Kitchen composters and worm composting bins are small, portable systems—these can be kept on a back porch or laundry room. In worm composting systems, red wriggler worms can make quick work of breaking down the food scraps for you—these are especially fun to have if there are kids in the house. And if you like to fish, you have a ready source of bait.

MULCHES

Mulches are protective layers applied to keep moisture from evaporating from the soil surface back into the air. They also reduce erosion and protect plant roots from high and low temperature extremes. In heavy clay soils, mulches can prevent the shrink-swell cycle that causes plants to be heaved up out of the ground. Additionally, they help keep dust down and can prevent weed germination. Spread over areas of bare soil, mulch gives new gardens with fewer, smaller plants a more uniform, filled-in appearance.

When it comes to mulch, deeper is not better! Deeper mulches deprive plant roots of oxygen and cause plants to smother. A 3" to 4" deep layer will do the trick. Keep mulch at least 2" away from the trunks of woody plants as it can cause crown and stem rot. Wood chips, compost pine needles, rock, gravel, straw, cotton hulls, and coconut fiber all make excellent mulches.

Inorganic mulches include rock, gravel, cinder, pumice, crushed limestone, and decomposed granite. Light-colored rocks reflect light and create reflected heat. Black rocks absorb heat and increase soil temperatures. If you are trying to moderate your microclimate to grow heat-loving plants, or to grow a plant that needs just a little more heat than local conditions provide, rock mulches can be used to warm the soil. They can also raise temperatures just enough to prevent leaf damage from light frosts. Be sure to consider how the mulch will look in your garden. Coral

The crushed rock mulch surrounding this wild four o'clock creates an attractive surface and warms the soil for speedy spring growth and heavy bloom.

pink rock may look fine in red-rock country, but the pink will shatter the visual harmony of a shaded woodland garden. The best colors of rock mulch are usually those that blend with your surroundings. Some gardeners use rock mulches to create dry streambeds in gardens. These are designed to create the illusion of water flowing through the landscape. Dry streambeds are lovely filled with ornamental grasses—they rustle nicely in the wind.

There are drawbacks to rock mulches. Inorganic mulches are very difficult to maintain and keep clean under pine, mesquite, acacia, aspen, or any other tree that drops flowers, leaves, or needles. Because it's hard to rake leaves and debris from mulches, many gardeners find the next step is to purchase a leaf-blower. Suddenly the peaceful garden activity, raking, has been replaced by loud and stinky leaf blowing. To avoid this, many gardeners limit mulching to the area within a deciduous tree's dripline and quietly groom the soil surface between plants with a metal leaf rake.

Many native plants are self-mulching, and care should be taken to let them do this job. For instance, the leaf mold and debris under mesquite plants is extremely rich in nitrogen and helps cool the soil. Other mulch products include cocoa hulls (beautiful, fragrant, but toxic to dogs if ingested) and coconut fiber. Think twice before you mulch with wood chips. They take a long time to break down (decades, perhaps even centuries) and will wash away in an instant with heavy rains. Rock, gravel, cinder, and even pine needles are better suited for use on slopes and areas that are subject to even occasional flooding.

If you find yourself with a large weedy area filled with difficult-to-eradicate weeds like foxtail and cheatgrass (grass that sticks in your socks), sheet-mulching may be the answer. First, water the weedy area thoroughly to a depth of 3". Next, lay down big sheets of cardboard—appliance boxes are great, but a collection of flattened smaller boxes or even thick sections of newspaper (soy inks, please) will do. Cover this with a 4" to 6" deep layer of manure or compost and water again until saturated. Next, top with a layer of straw, leaves, or grass clippings to hold in the moisture. Within six months your weeds will be gone and you can dig holes through the sheet mulch still in place and plant.

FERTILIZER

Most southwestern plants benefit from an annual dose of fertilizer. Be conservative about how much and how frequently you fertilize. Add too much, and luxury consumption will result in overly succulent, disease- and insect-prone plants. (You'll read more about that later on.)

Each spring, I dig composted manure into the top 6" of soil around every perennial plant in my garden. This gives their growth a boost, helps open up the soil so that water and air can enter and circulate, and supplies the soil with a little organic matter. For most southwestern plants, this is all the fertilizer they'll ever need. Exceptions to this treatment are cacti and dry-loving denizens of lean-mineral soils. These plants can take an application of weak balanced fertilizer to boost growth, but no organic matter. Be sure to apply fertilizer early enough in the season for growth to harden off before summer heat (February in desert gardens, May at mid-elevations) and winter cold (August) in high-elevation zones.

■ The Right Plants: Native, Adaptive, and Xeric

The Southwest is enormous and has many gardening environments. The plant profiles section to follow features beautiful, easy-to-grow plants for this region and points out some of the outstanding characteristics that make them great choices. Not every plant featured will be a good choice for every garden. Check each plant's USDA climate zone, sun and soil needs, and moisture requirements to decide which are right for you.

Keeping plants from drying out is the number-one gardening challenge here in the Southwest. Choosing the right plants for each location, making sure they get adequate water, and applying mulch to keep water from evaporating are the three ways to meet this challenge. The amount of water each plant needs will vary with local conditions. A plant that rarely needs watering in a cool part of town may need regular water in a hotter, more open location. Will you water once a day, once a week, or once in a blue moon? Determine this before you buy your plants, and pick only plants that will do well with the care you'll give. Those yellow stream monkeyflowers are lovely, but don't get talked into planting too many water-loving plants or you'll have to take out a second mortgage to pay the water bill.

If you're starting a new garden or making major changes to an established garden, the first plants you'll want to choose will be functional plants: deciduous trees to plant on southern and western exposures to cool your home in the summer, perhaps even as a patio umbrella, and then to let you bask in the winter sun after they shed their leaves. If possible, you'll want to build patios and outdoor living spaces according to climate—a patio on the north side of the house gives you a cool outdoor living space in hot desert summers. High in the cool mountain pines, you will want to put your patio on the south side of the house for maximum warmth.

Whether hot or cold, winds take their toll on plants. Southwestern springs and falls are nearly always very windy. Summers and winters can also be windy. Planting trees or shrubs for windbreaks or situating buildings, walls, and pieces of hardscape where they will block winds can help protect your plants. Shrubs, vines, and large perennials can also soften the look of hard walls anywhere. They tone down reflected sun in hot deserts. Once you've moderated the impacts of sun and wind, the rest of your planting will be much easier.

If your garden has existing woody plants, take the time to evaluate them and decide if they meet your needs. Large plants may have taken many, many years to reach their current size and have value as long as they're not bringing old problems forward into your new garden. A good rule is not to remove any existing plant in your garden until you figure out whether it's a weed or a durable native. Only time will tell if that undistinguished little green mound will burst into glorious bloom with the advent of the first monsoon.

Our southwestern sun is so bright that many plants traditionally planted in full sun will grow in partial shade or filtered light. But they may not bloom or produce fruit in locations with less sun. Fruit-bearing plants like tomatoes and oranges need full sun to manufacture fruits. Many sun-loving perennials also need bright sun for full bloom. Heavenly bamboo and star jasmine are two of the many plants that need full sunlight in more moderate climates; however, they will scorch in hot desert summers unless they are given cool exposures or filtered light. Regardless of geographic location, shade plants always need shade. If there's not a hint of shade in your yard now, wait for those trees you just planted to cast some significant shadows before you plant your shade-loving ground cover beneath. In the meantime, plant a fast-growing, sun-loving annual or ground cover now, and be prepared to replace it as trees grow and create shade.

WHAT TYPE OF GARDEN DO YOU WANT? FORMAL VERSUS NATURALISTIC GARDENS

Formal gardens are highly structured. They rely heavily on hardscape, strong lines, and a high degree of organization. Plants in formal gardens can seem more like sculpture than living beings, or can be arranged in blocks of color like paint to convey a desired effect. Naturalistic gardens mimic nature in appearance and structure. Informal gardens utilize mixed beds and borders with plants in seemingly casual (but usually highly orchestrated) drifts.

USING NATIVE AND ADAPTED PLANTS

No matter what garden style you choose, your plant selection can include native plants, adapted plants, and drought-tolerant plants. Native plants are the locals—they've been living untended in the area for as long as anybody can remember—frequently for thousands of years. In an environment as varied as the Southwest, there are many native plant habitats.

You may be surprised to find that not all native plants are drought-tolerant. Knowing where a particular native plant can grow in the wild will help you decide if it is a good choice for your garden. In the introduction, you read about native plants found on the plains. Some of these plants, like blanket flowers (*Gaillardia* species) and prairie clovers (*Dalea* species), are also native in the Southwest. Because of our varied topography, many other native plant habitats besides the plains exist in the Southwest. To find out which wild species grow in your region, contact your local native plant society (see Resources section).

Adapted plants come from geographically distant locations, but grow in southwestern gardens without a lot of fuss. Typically, they come from other parts of the world with similar climates and soils. Both native and adapted plants can be drought-tolerant. Water needs are always relative to planting location, and which plants are "drought-tolerant" depends on where they are planted. A low water use plant from Albuquerque might be a moderate or high water user in the southern Arizona desert.

Two strategies help plants survive drought, and you'll probably want to have plants with both strategies in your garden. Some plants avoid drought, and others tolerate it. Drought-avoiders grow actively when water is abundant—think of annual wildflowers, spring bulbs, and summer deciduous native plants. Drought-tolerators are plants that can continue normal growth under dry conditions—they grow, flower, and set seed during periods when drought can be expected. Red bird-of-paradise, banana yucca, and tufted evening primrose all not only grow, but thrive in hot, dry conditions. Some plants go beyond drought tolerance—"xerophilic," or dry-loving plants, can only survive in dry conditions. These can be killed by kindness, in the form of overwatering or watering during the dry season.

PLANTS FOR FIRE-WISE GARDENS

If you live in a fire-prone area, or at the urban-wildlands interface, you'll want to incorporate fire safety into your garden design and plant selection. To create and maintain a fire-safe landscape, you need to consider what type of plants you install, how far they are spaced from

CACTI AND SUCCULENTS—LOW-WATER FAVORITES

Of all the drought-adapted plants, cacti and succulents have the most interesting structure. Their striking forms and succulent leaves have evolved as adaptations for water storage in arid conditions. Cacti have reduced leaves, jointed cylindrical stems or pads, and large, often brilliant, many-petaled flowers. Some have spines. Succulence, the ability to store water in plant tissues, is found in many other plants than cacti. Agaves, yuccas, aloes, hesperaloes, ocotillos, live-forevers, and ice plants are all succulents. Many cacti and succulents come from deserts throughout the world. Others are tender tropicals, seashore species, or mountain dwellers. To select cacti and succulents for year-round outdoor growing, consult the USDA hardiness zones.

Most cacti and succulents make good container specimens. If you live in a cold zone, try growing cacti in pots. Cacti grow best in a mixture of sand, silt, and gravel. Other succulents need a well-drained potting mixture—mix one part potting soil, one part sand or native soil, and one part pumice. Lacking the extensive root systems they would form if planted in the ground, most container-grown succulents should not be placed in full sun. If you move indoor-grown cacti and succulents outside for the winter, be sure to move them gradually from shade to partial sun or they will be damaged. Plants will burn unless they are acclimatized to sunlight. ■

your home and other plants, and how you take care of them. To create a defensible zone around your house, plant low-growing and fire-resistant species. Avoid plants with high resin content (e.g., pines, junipers, and sumacs) and plants with a dense, woody growth habit. It's only natural to treasure trees and the shade they create, but please remember that no trees or woody plants should be planted under roof eaves or within 10' of your home in forested or chaparral areas. Woody plants should also be spaced far apart, with branches trimmed to at least 6' from the ground.

Drought-tolerant plants with small leaves reduce a fire's fuel volume. Succulent plants and the leaves of deciduous plants generally have a high moisture content, which reduces their flammability. Many salt-tolerant plants have natural fire resistance. Fire-adapted native species will resprout after a fire passes through and can prevent soil erosion after fire. Herbaceous wildflowers and flowering perennials are always good choices for fire-wise gardens.

Garden maintenance is at least as important as the plants you select and where you place them. Routinely rake up and dispose of needles, plant litter, and debris. All plants within 150' of the house should be well maintained and well watered, and all dead plant material regularly removed. Keep dense growth thinned, remove dead and damaged branches, and trim lower branches to at least 6' from the ground on all woody plants. Use inorganic materials for paths and mulches. Pine needles, wood chips, and bark can ignite and spread fire to your home.

PLANTS FOR FIRE-WISE GARDENS

In combination with regular watering, meticulous maintenance, and good plant spacing, selection of the least flammable plants can boost your garden's fire resistance. Some suggestions follow. See the Resources section and check with your local fire department for specific requirements for your area.

SUCCULENTS
Agave (*Agave* species)
Beargrass (*Nolina* species)

CACTUS
Red hesperaloe (*Hesperaloe parviflora*)
Stone-crop (*Sedum* species)
Yucca (*Yucca* species)

LOW-GROWING GROUND COVERS
Blue grama (*Bouteloua gracilis*)
Cooper's ice plant (*Delosperma cooperi*)
Creeping mahonia (*Mahonia repens*)
Galleta (*Pleuraphis jamesii*)
Hardy yellow ice plant (*Delosperma nubigenum*)
Meadow rue (*Thalictrum fendleri*)
Mexican evening primrose (*Oenothera speciosa*)
Prairie smoke (*Geum triflorum*)
Pussytoes (*Antennaria* species)

Rosea ice plant (*Drosanthemum floribundum*)
Silver cinquefoil (*Potentilla hippiana*)
Silver dead-nettle (*Lamium maculatum*)
Snow-in-summer (*Cerastium tomentosum*)
Soapwort (*Saponaria ocymoides*)
Spring cinquefoil (*Potentilla verna*)
Virginia creeper (*Parthenocissus virginiana*)
Wild grape (*Vitis arizonica*)
Wine cup (*Callirhoe involucrata*)
Yarrow (*Achillea millefolium*)

FIRE-RESISTANT SHRUBS AND TREES
Apache plume (*Fallugia paradoxa*)
Aspen (*Populus tremuloides*)
Desert olive (*Forestiera pubescens*)
Desert willow (*Chilopsis linearis*)
Four-wing saltbush (*Atriplex canescens*)
Fremont barberry (*Mahonia fremontii*)
Golden currant (*Ribes aureum*)
Japanese barberry (*Berberis thunbergii*)
Ocotillo (*Fouquieria splendens*)
Oregon grape (*Mahonia aquifolium*)
Palms (*Washingtonia, Brahea, Phoenix,*
   and *Chamaerops* species)
Redbud (*Cercis* species)
Red-twig dogwood (*Cornus stolonifera*)
Rose (*Rosa* species)
Shrub cinquefoil (*Potentilla fruticosa*) ■

Cacti, standing like sentinels along this straight garden path, point the way to a bright bougainvillea and inviting hacienda.

■ Hardscape—The Great Organizer

No matter how well you plan your plantings, there will be times when hardscape is the element that holds everything together. Well-designed paths help organize gardens and also provide areas of a garden that always look good with only occasional maintenance. If you are working in an existing garden, check to make sure its paths serve your current needs and take you where you need to go. Our natural tendency is to travel the shortest distance between two points. Paths laid out that ignore this behavior are often abandoned for more direct routes. If your garden is a blank slate, you will want to give serious consideration to where your paths will be placed, how wide they will be, and what materials they will be made of. Traffic patterns will help you determine the widths and surface textures of the paths and their placement.

Garden Paths

First off, think about where you will want to walk in the garden, what equipment you will need to transport on paths, and any special needs you may have. If you're uncertain about any of this, stake out temporary paths and see how well they meet your needs before you commit to a particular path layout. Primary paths, designed so that two adults can walk side by side, are usually at least 5' wide, but not all home gardens are of large enough scale for paths of this size. Secondary paths, 3' wide, allow for passage of wheelbarrows, carts, and lawnmowers.

Paths can be soft or hard. Soft paths are easy to install, but require greater upkeep. Edges of the path should be defined by flexible edging and the surface of the path should be neatly raked. Creating a soft path can be as simple as laying down cinder, crushed rock, gravel,

**Pavers form a neat edging along this curving, informal garden path.
Garden perennials are arranged to mirror the shapes and arrangements of the adjacent wild plant community.**

decomposed granite, chipped wood, or sand; spreading it to a uniform depth; and raking it smooth. In sandy desert areas, such a path creates an inexpensive walkway that prevents people from compacting soil in growing areas and guides them through the garden.

A good garden path reflects the needs of its caretakers. If you like to walk barefoot or pad around in flip-flops, for instance, rough-edged rocks and loose stones are probably not the best surface. Instead, try decomposed granite, coarse play sand, or a living path of mowed yarrow. My good friends Olga and Marshall are schoolteachers with no kids at home—they installed a simple circular gravel path, then seeded it with hundreds of tiny polished stones and unusual rocks purchased on annual treks to Quartzite, Arizona. When friends with children come to visit, the kids are turned out on a treasure hunt to see what they can find, leaving the adults free to socialize and relax. At the end of the evening, each child has the joy of picking one treasure to keep and returns the rest of the stones to the path for the next round of visitors.

Cost is a major consideration when planning paths and walkways. Hard paths usually cost far more than soft paths. But hard paths can be created inexpensively from stabilized soft paths—

paths of decomposed gravel, cinder, or crushed rock that are firmed with a roller and hardened with a fixative. Paths and pads can be made of pavers, stones, bricks, deck material, poured concrete, wood, or rock. Grass pavers are honeycombs that provide structural support for traffic but allow water to filter through their surface. Path materials vary by locality—look for local materials with colors and textures that complement your home and surroundings. Depending on where you live, sandstone, limestone, flagstone, granite, cinder, river rock, adobe brick, and basalt are available.

Think, too, of your special needs. Some friends just put a lovely path of homemade molded concrete cobbles and sand on the side of their house. I don't know whether or not it was their intention, but they will never again easily roll their trash container to their back yard for spring cleanup. If you expect visits from a family member with a walker, baby carriage, or wheelchair, smooth, even surfaces will enable your guest to move about more freely.

Another neighbor has installed a boardwalk. I love the old-fashioned look of this path and the way it makes use of recycled lumber. There's a lot of heavy labor involved in installing hardscape, so take time to choose a durable material you'll be happy to live with. Whatever material you choose, make sure paths are graded to shed water and are free of low spots that accumulate puddles and dirt. Paths can be slanted slightly to channel water to garden beds during downpours.

Garden Walls and Other Structures

Walls define a garden space, serve as the border for raised planters, and provide shelter from heat, cold, and wind. In hot areas, they can be cooled and softened by plants. In many gardens, beautifully crafted stone walls and brightly painted fences are an attraction in their own right, with or without flowers in bloom. Low stacked rock walls and planters are easy to build—try using rocks from a local source. Adobe walls, wrought-iron work, and ceramic tiles are regional specialties. Straw-bale walls covered with earth plaster or stucco will impart a timeless, flowing, handmade feeling to your garden room—and they're inexpensive and relatively easy to build.

Arbors, trellises, and pergolas are garden structures that can be covered with vines to create lush green garden rooms. Even in a small patio, you can create a soothing bower by training fast-growing vines like Virginia creeper, desert grape, wild clematis, or rose to climb up an arbor or shade ramada. Vine-covered structures give a marvelously comforting sense of enclosure—there's something primal about our need for these "secret garden" spaces, so give one a try.

Sometimes, no matter how carefully I've planned, there are times of the year when nothing is particularly eye-catching in my garden. (I know I'm not supposed to admit this, but I'm sharing

EASY-TO-GROW HERBS FOR CONTAINER GARDENS

FOR THE CAT—catnip, catmint, annual ryegrass, wheatgrass

FOR THE COOK—oregano, basil, thyme, bay laurel, rosemary, spearmint, cooking sage, chives, parsley

FOR THE TEAPOT—apple mint, lemon balm, chamomile, chocolate mint, pineapple sage, lemon grass

FOR THE SWEET TOOTH—stevia, sweet cicely, licorice hyssop

FOR FRAGRANCE AND BEAUTY—lavender, calendula, miniature roses, costmary, mugwort, lemon verbena

An arrangement of clay pots of golden barrel cacti, columnar cacti, and agaves provides structure, gives a sense of enclosure, and forms a low wall in this sunny high-desert garden.

because you'll have times like these too!) Before I discovered containers, I'd panic when guests were coming over and exhaust myself trying to beat the garden into tip-top shape. No longer! Thanks to my nongardening friends, I've discovered the magic of containers. Keep a few moderate- and large-sized containers on hand—terra-cotta or glazed pottery will do the trick—as well as several large bags of potting soil and some Spanish moss or rounded stones for surface dressing. Next, run to the nursery and buy an assortment of fully blooming complementary plants, plug them into the pots, and place these in prominent locations. Voilà, instant color without backbreaking labor! Finally, sit back and enjoy the party. Containers are also an easy way to decorate your public space and define the path to your front door. Try planting durable bunch-grasses, succulents, and evergreen shrubs that will weather the hottest and coldest times of the year and still look great!

Most herbs thrive in container gardens. Try planting several large pots, and many smaller ones, with all of your favorites. Container herb gardens make welcome gifts as well—particularly for housewarming celebrations, for cooks, and for the person who has everything.

■ Garden Practices

WATERING WITH CARE

Summer rains are often torrential, and without specific action for their capture or delay, their precious water can be quickly lost by runoff. Rain barrels, downspouts, and cisterns are all devices used to capture rainfall and save it for drier times. Gray-water systems direct used household water from sinks and washing machines to non–food-producing parts of the garden. Utilizing natural grades, sloping paved surfaces toward planted areas, and creating swales and contours are other means to direct or channel water. With water in the Southwest so hard to come by, learning how to make the most of it is a critical gardening skill.

The two best ways of supplying water to plants are basin and drip irrigation. The lushest plants you'll see growing in dry gardens are always the ones on drip irrigation. Simple drip systems are easy to install. Because they put water right where it is needed, at each plant's rootzone, they can't be beat for water-use efficiency. To build an uncomplicated hose-end system, you need only a pressure regulator, drip hose, tubing, and emitters. Install systems above ground, then cover with mulch. Take the time to walk your drip lines each time you water to be sure they are working right. If you don't want to install a drip system, basin irrigation also works well. (Rob Proctor provided instructions for this in the introduction.) Build a planting basin around each new plant or group of plants. To water, fill the basin with several inches of water. Whether you choose a drip system or basin irrigation, be sure to mulch.

Each plant's need for water varies as it grows and matures, and also changes with the weather. To get a handle on whether or not your plants need water, buy a water meter—an inexpensive one ($3 to $6) from the local discount store will do for open, rock-free garden soils. If your soils are heavy or rocky you'll need to get a heavy-duty model ($20 to $25). Water dry-loving plants only when the meter indicates soils are at the low limits of "moist." If you use drip irrigation, make sure your emitter volume is adjustable. As plants mature, their water needs will change and you can adjust the flow on each plant individually. Also, be prepared to move the irrigation zone out farther as the plants' roots extend out from their rootballs into the surrounding soil.

As a general rule, avoid watering during the heat of the day. Hoses and irrigation systems filled with hot water will cook roots. Water passing through hot soils and over hot rocks can steam your roots. Except when you are washing off dust, avoid getting water on plant leaves, especially during the evening or in the shade. For many plants, shade plus water on leaves equals powdery mildew, a difficult-to-eliminate, disfiguring white fungus.

Some traditional southwestern gardening techniques adapt ancient technology to modern needs. To conserve water, lower planting beds several inches from the surrounding areas. This technique (based on Zuni waffle gardens) helps collect rainfall and deliver it where it can do the most good. If you have deep soil, you might consider planting a sunken garden. The cooling effects of soil depth and shading from walls help reduce plant water needs.

Grouping plants with similar water needs also conserves both water and energy. To make the best use of water, group plants according to their water needs and put plants that need the most water (vegetables, cutting gardens, and fruit trees) close to your house, where you'll be sure to see them and give them the attention they require. You won't have to go walking all the way out to the garden's edge to pick a rose or gather some basil for dinner.

COPING WITH CRITTERS

Wherever you live in the Southwest, you are surrounded by wildlife. Because of this, gardening opportunities and gardening trials abound. Javelina, deer, rabbits, elk, ground squirrels, skunks, pack rats, gophers, mice, birds, and grasshoppers can wreak major havoc on gardens. To end up with anything at all growing in your garden, you will need to protect young plants from local wildlife.

If you can't fence the entire garden, be sure to protect young plants with wire caging or individual fencing. I know one experienced Sedona gardener who recommends caging new plants (including perennials and baby cactus) with ½" mesh hardware cloth—a 50' roll will make 100 9" by 24" cages. For larger woody plants, chicken-wire cylinders left on for two years will allow them to develop enough growth to resist damage by javelinas, deer, pack rats, and rabbits. The length of time it takes to protect plants varies with the plants and animals concerned. Quaking aspen trees need protection until their leaves are above 8' height, the height most elk can reach.

If you've ever seen a plant suddenly pulled down into the ground and disappear, you've seen a gopher in action. Gophers leave mounds of churned-up soil in their wake—you walk outside in the morning and wonder who's been plowing the garden. Ground squirrels also target plants from below but frequently eat only underground parts, leaving tops behind to wilt and die. Rabbits confine their plant-eating activities to above-ground portions.

In one ground squirrel– and rabbit-laden garden, we planted all of our perennials with wire cages both above and below ground level. To do this yourself, first dig a hole, bury one wire cage deep enough that 1" extends just above the soil, fill the cage with a little dirt, and then

HUMMINGBIRD PLANTS

Did you know that 17 species of hummingbirds can be found in the Southwest? Hummingbirds are the smallest birds, known for their iridescent feathers, lightning-quick darting flight, and hovering feeding patterns. Their needle-like beaks and long tongues allow them to extract nectar from deep-throated flowers. Red is their favorite flower color, but they are also attracted to orange, yellow, pink, and purple blooms. Predominantly nectar feeders, they also eat aphids, small insects, and spiders. Hummingbird nests built on vertical branches of trees, shrubs, and vines are tiny cups, sometimes decorated with lichen, leaves, or cottony fibers. Following are 20 gorgeous plants to attract hummingbirds to your garden:

COMMON NAME	SCIENTIFIC NAME	SUN/SHADE	ZONES
Baja fairy duster	Calliandra californica	Sun	9–11
Balsam	Impatiens	Shade/sun	All
California fuchsia	Zauschneria californica	Sun	6–10
Chuparosa	Justicia californica	Sun	10–11
Claret cup cactus	Echinocereus triglochidiatus	Sun	5–9
Coral bell	Heuchera sanguinea	Shade/sun	All
Desert willow	Chilopsis linearis	Sun	6–11
Eaton's firecracker	Penstemon eatonii	Sun	5–11
Firebush	Hamelia patens	Sun	8–11
Flame honeysuckle	Anisacanthus quadrifidus var. wrightii	Sun/partial shade	8–11
Four o'clock	Mirabilis species	Sun/partial shade	All
Golden columbine	Aquilegia chrysantha	Shade/sun	All
Lavender	Lavandula species	Sun	5–11
Mexican sage	Salvia leucantha	Sun	10–11
Red bird-of-paradise	Caesalpinia pulcherrima	Sun	9–11
Red-hot poker	Kniphofia uvaria	Sun	4–9
Rocky Mountain bee plant	Cleome serrulata	Sun	All
Sunset hyssop	Agastache rupestris	Sun	5–11
Trumpet creeper	Campsis radicans	Sun/partial shade	All
Western redbud	Cercis species	Sun	5–11
Yellow bell	Tecoma stans	Sun	9–11

place the plant in the cage. After planting, wire the top cage securely to the bottom one. The top cage can be removed after the first or second growing season; the bottom one stays in place. Planting bulbs in subterranean wire baskets and lining flowerbeds with hardware cloth will also thwart gophers. Some gardeners swear that daffodil bulbs planted around young fruit trees repel gophers. Another strategy for small mammal control is exclusion. Fencing the perimeter of your garden will keep out skunks, gophers, prairie dogs, and pocket gophers. You will need to install small poultry mesh in a 3' deep trench as well as fencing above ground to do this effectively.

If you find the tips of many plants vanishing from your garden, suspect a pack rat. These fascinating animals often gather substantial collections of plant parts and found items. A friend of mine kept her vacuum cleaner in an outdoor storage shed surrounded by piñon juniper woodland. One day she found it in the midst of a pack rat arrangement that resembled a medieval altar. They are wily, super smart, and hard to deter. Keeping a dog or cat may discourage pack rats. King snakes and garter snakes also provide excellent rodent control.

ATTRACTING WILDLIFE

Although your new plants will be better off with some animals securely kept out of your garden, you'll want to encourage beneficial creatures, such as birds and butterflies. A large garden provides the best habitat. However, you can still be a wildlife gardener with only a small patio or balcony, where carefully selected container plants can attract and nourish hummingbirds, songbirds, hawk moths, and butterflies.

To attract wanted wildlife to your garden, you need to provide the basic necessities of life— food, water, and shelter. Also, have a wholesome, pesticide- and herbicide-free environment. Depending on who'll be dining, foods include nectar, pollen, seeds, fruits, spiders, and insects. Provide what you can with plants, then supplement with feeders. Both butterflies and hummingbirds are nectar feeders. Unless you live in their winter territory, you'll want to take down hummingbird feeders as soon as fall temperatures drop. Birdseed should be provided year-round.

BUTTERFLY PLANTS

Butterflies are drawn to sunny gardens, and they like to sunbathe on warm rocks. You may need nectar plants for adults and food plants for caterpillars to draw them to your garden. Butterflies make particularly good use of the feeding platforms of large, flat flowers. Some of the showier common groups of flowering garden plants that feed caterpillars and attract butterflies include:

Asters—Fleabane, coneflower, globe thistle, yarrow, coreopsis, sunflower, brittlebush
Butterfly bushes (*Buddleia* species)
Mallows—hollyhock
Milkweeds (*Asclepias* species)
Mints—desert lavender, spearmint, Agastache, bee balm, lemon balm, rosemary
Mustards—wallflower, candytuft, alyssum
Peas—lupine, sweet pea, wisteria, locust, mesquite
Pinks—carnation, cottage pink, sea thrift
Roses—Spirea, Caryopteris, flowering crabapple, wild rose
Snapdragons—penstemon, snapdragon, foxglove, Texas ranger
Wild buckwheats (*Eriogonum* species)

Large rocks for basking lizards and butterflies and a variety of nectar-bearing flowers are the heart of this wildlife-friendly garden.

Birds need clean water for bathing and drinking—and butterflies need shallow water. You can make a nice mud wallow for butterflies by placing a dish-type planter filled with soil in a saucer of water.

To shelter creatures from the elements, you can install bird and bat houses. Trees, shrubs, and vines all provide nesting sites as well., Large rocks for basking in the sun and piles of rock for shelter will give you the best chance of attracting and keeping reptiles in your garden. Because lizards, snakes, and other reptiles eat many times their weight in insects, they can be very beneficial to your garden. They're also fascinating to watch and (except for rattlers and Gila monsters) a whole lot of fun to have around.

PLANTS WITH BERRIES AND SEEDS TO ATTRACT BIRDS AND WILDLIFE

Berries and seeds are major food sources for birds and small animals. Try some of these in your garden.

BERRIES
Black chokeberry (*Aronia melanocarpa*)
Cotoneaster (*Cotoneaster* species)
Currant and gooseberry (*Ribes* species)
Elderberry (*Sambucus* species)
Firethorn (*Pyracantha*)
Heavenly bamboo (*Nandina* species)
Honeysuckle (*Lonicera* species)
Littleleaf sumac, three-leaf sumac, sugarbush
   (*Rhus* species)

Manzanita and kinnikinnick (*Arctostaphylos* species)
Oregon grape, Fremont barberry, red barberry
   (*Mahonia* species)
Rose hips (*Rosa* species)
Virginia creeper (*Parthenocissus virginiaca*)
Wild grape (*Vitis* species)
Wild plum (*Prunus americanus*)

SEEDS AND NUTS
Native grass
Oak (acorns)
Palm
Pinyon pine (pine nuts)
Quailbush (*Atriplex lentiformis*)

■ Plants for Success

PERENNIALS

✿

MOONSHINE YARROW
Achillea filipendulina 'Moonshine'
Category: sun perennial
Use: for border, in butterfly garden
Soil: any; best with good drainage
Hardiness: all zones
Mature size: 18" by 24"

With its silver-gray fern-like foliage and large, flat, lemon-yellow flower clusters, moonshine yarrow is one of the most elegant low water–use garden perennials. Like all yarrows, it has a long blooming period. Its flowers, arranged in spreading umbrella-shaped clusters (called umbels), are a favorite perch for butterflies and can be cut for fresh bouquets or dried arrange-

---

Moonshine yarrow (*Achillea filipendulina* 'Moonshine')

ments. Once established, moonshine yarrow is unrivaled in its ease of care and can be watered frequently or rarely with equal success. Yarrow does best in full sun in cooler areas, but takes filtered light or partial shade in hot deserts.

Plant moonshine yarrow in drifts with other butterfly-attracting plants—blue-flowered salvias and veronicas, tall phlox (*Phlox paniculata*), butterfly bush (*Buddleia davidii*), and silver-leafed Russian sage (*Perovskia atriplicifolia*). Or combine moonshine yarrow with 'Dark Knight' spirea (*Caryopteris clandonensis* 'Dark Knight') and *Euonymus fortunei* 'Emerald and Gold' in a simple low water–use planting. Its divided leaves and gently mounding form help soften the appearance of gravel and crushed-rock surfaces. The entire plant has a fresh, meadowy scent.

Moonshine yarrow attracts a host of pollinators to the garden. Remove old flower stems to encourage repeated blooms. Another *Achillea filipendulina* cultivar, 'Coronation Gold', grows to 3' tall with bright yellow flower clusters.

A related species, fernleaf yarrow (*Achillea millefolium*) has fragrant, finely divided bright green leaves topped by many clusters of small white flowers and makes a wonderful fragrant lawn substitute. Fernleaf yarrow cultivars provide many flower colors: 'Cerise Queens' are bright red, 'Paprikas' brick red, and 'Roseas' light pink.

Potential problems: divide overly large or crowded clumps in fall.

HOLLYHOCK
Alcea rosea
Category: sun biennial or short-lived perennial
Use: for background or tall border
Soil: any with regular watering
Hardiness: all zones
Mature size: 3' to 6' (but up to 9') tall by 2' wide

Hollyhocks are an old-fashioned garden favorite. They have an upright growth habit, hand-sized rough green leaves, and tall spikes of many 3" to 6" wide five-petaled flowers in white, red, pink, burgundy, pale yellow, or apricot. They do best with regular water, but are not fussy and can be neglected without dire consequence. Deer may avoid browsing on their hairy leaves.

Hollyhocks bloom in summer; flowers open first at the bottom of the flower spike and progress upward throughout the growing season. Plant them with other tall, old-fashioned perennials like butterfly bushes, tall foxgloves, Russell hybrid lupines, sunflowers, annual cosmos, gladiolus, and hibiscus, and watch the hummingbirds and butterflies come. Hollyhocks come in double-petaled and single-petaled forms and can be annual, biennial, or perennial. 'Chater's Doubles' is a 6' tall perennial strain with 5" to 6" wide flowers. Black hollyhocks have incredible dark maroon flowers that appear nearly black.

It is easy to collect hollyhock seeds, held on the plant in round cheesewheels in autumn; wear gloves to protect hands from irritating hairs when picking these. Seeds can be stored and broadcast in spring, or left to fall and naturalize. Hollyhocks will self-sow if seeds are allowed to drop; however, double forms may not come true from seed. Volunteers (seedlings that sprout without cultivation) are easy to dig and can be moved to permanent locations in spring.

Potential problems: hollyhocks are prone to rust; infected leaves should be removed and taken out of the garden. Snails, slugs, and grasshoppers all like hollyhocks' thick leaves—try putting out saucers of beer at dusk to lure these nibblers to their drunken doom.

Hollyhock (*Alcea rosea*)

ABOVE: Golden columbine (*Aquilegia chrysantha*)
BELOW: Butterfly milkweed (*Asclepias tuberosa*)

GOLDEN COLUMBINE
Aquilegia chrysantha
Category: sun or shade perennial
Use: for borders, mass planting, or in containers
Soil: any with regular watering
Hardiness: all zones
Mature size: 1' to 3' by 1' to 2'

Golden columbines grow in sun or shade. They are covered with large 3" to 4" long spurred yellow flowers held on tall stems above dappled light-green, maidenhair fern–like leaves, First bloom occurs in late spring, with another flush of flowers just after the heat of summer. Hummingbirds visit columbines regularly.

In hot desert areas, give columbines regular water and protection from afternoon sun. Keep roots moist and cool with a 3" layer of organic mulch. Newly planted columbines require frequent watering, but become increasingly drought tolerant as they grow.

Columbines make a great ground cover for dry shade and mix well with other shade perennials. Interplant the spaces between golden columbines with spring-flowering bulbs of yellow, white, pink, lavender, and blue—hyacinths, daffodils, tulips, and Siberian squills are good choices. Because columbines are so easy to grow and bloom so reliably, they are great container plants.

Hybrid columbines combine colors in enchanting combinations; strains include long-spurred 'McKana Giants' and compact 'Beidermeier' hybrids (1' tall). Compact varieties can be planted as an edging or in rock gardens. One outstanding golden columbine variety, 'Swallowtail', is a large-flowered 3' tall by 18" wide cultivar discovered in Pima County, Arizona. Rocky Mountain columbine (*Aquilegia caerulea*), Colorado's state flower, has erect blue and white flowers. Desert columbine (*Aquilegia desertorum*) is a drought-tolerant species with nodding orange-red flowers and compact gray-green leaves. Columbines will readily cross-breed. To maintain plants true to species, plant only one type of columbine, or do not allow plants to self-seed.

Potential problems: some strains are susceptible to powdery mildew.

BUTTERFLY MILKWEED
Asclepias tuberosa
Category: sun perennial
Use: in dry garden, butterfly garden, and as color accent
Soil: any with low to moderate watering
Hardiness: all zones
Mature size: 2' by 2'

Butterfly milkweed comes in two forms, one with bright orange flowers, the other bright yellow. (To make sure you get the color you want, buy plants in bloom.) Shiny, fragrant flowers look like spurred crowns borne in dense, flat-topped 3" wide clusters at every branch tip. Their fragrance attracts many butterfly species (including monarchs), honeybees, and hummingbirds. To keep butterflies coming, create a garden of butterfly-attracting species with a succession of blooms—asters, fleabanes, salvias, monardas, sedums, coneflowers, and wallflowers. Other plants that mix well with showy milkweed are penstemons, globe mallows, and blanket flowers.

Butterfly milkweed should be planted in well-drained soils in full sun; it blooms in midsummer. Removing first flowers after bloom will prolong the flowering season and help plants remain compact and full.

For desert gardens, another milkweed to try is desert milkweed (*Asclepias subulata*), a drought-tolerant native southwestern perennial, with nearly leafless stems and creamy white flowers throughout summer, that grows to 4' high by 2' wide. Water once a month in summer.

Pineleaf milkweed (*Asclepias linaria*) is a 2' by 3' perennial with small white summer blooms atop a rounded evergreen shrub with needle-like leaves. The flowers develop into inflated ornamental seedpods in early fall. Plant pineleaf milkweed in a sunny spot where it will receive protection from afternoon heat.

For upland gardens, try showy milkweed (*Asclepias speciosa*), an upright, coarse-textured 3½' by 4' spreading perennial with light gray-green leaves and huge spectacular clusters of 1" star-shaped rose-pink flowers.

Potential problems: aphids frequent butterfly milkweeds and turn orange when they feed on its sap. These can be washed off.

PURPLE CONEFLOWER
Echinacea purpurea
Category: sun perennial
Use: for borders, in butterfly garden
Soil: any soil that's not soggy; does well in alkaline soils
Hardiness: all zones
Mature size: 2' to 4' by 2' to 3'

Purple coneflower is an elegant, sturdy, long-blooming perennial. It boasts many 3" to 4" diameter flowers on upright stems above oblong, deep green leaves. In desert areas, purple coneflowers bloom from late spring to early summer. They are best sited in filtered sunlight in the coolest location you can find. At higher elevations in full sun, bloom lasts from midsummer into autumn. Flowers may reach a height of 4' on plants in loose, rich soil with ample water.

Butterflies and bees visit newly opened coneflowers for nectar. In autumn, birds eat purple coneflower seeds. Purple coneflowers are prairie natives, and at mid to high elevations they can be seeded in an informal wildflower meadow of prairie grasses and wildflowers, including little bluestem (*Schizachryium scoparium*), prairie dropseed (*Sporobolus heterolepsis*), prairie purple coneflower (*Echinacea angustifolia*), purple prairie clover (*Petalostemon purpureum*), blackfoot daisy (*Melampodium leucanthum*), and dwarf sundrop (*Calylophus serrulatus*).

Purple coneflowers need regular water the first two years of growth but become moderately drought tolerant once established. Plant coneflowers 3' apart to allow for their slowly spreading growth habit. They can be divided in fall after three or more years' growth.

Two of the best coneflower varieties are 'Magnus' (2" to 4" by 18"), with large reddish-purple petals forming flat rays around the cone, and 'White Swan', a heavy-blooming compact (2' to

2½' tall by 2' wide) cultivar with gorgeous 4" flowerheads of white reflexed petals and a large golden cone.

Potential problems: overwatering and soggy soils can seriously stunt their growth, and if waterlogging persists, plants will die. To prevent powdery mildew, avoid getting water on leaves.

Purple coneflower (*Echinacea purpurea*)

ABOVE: Rockrose (*Helianthemum nummularium*)
BELOW: Coral bells (*Heuchera sanguinea*)

ROCKROSE
Helianthemum nummularium
Category: sun perennial or subshrub
Use: as border or small area ground cover; in rock gardens and containers
Soil: any soil with good drainage
Hardiness: all zones
Mature size: 6" to 8" high x 3' wide

Rockrose is an evergreen plant for the reflected heat and mineral soils of the rocky Southwest. It is a prolific bloomer, covered in clusters of 1" flowers of yellow, rose, apricot, white, red, orange, peach, or salmon. Although each flower lasts for only one day, new buds keep opening for an entire month or longer. Most of its plants have a neat mounding or mat-like form with gray or green leaves.

Rockrose puts on the best floral display when planted in full sun, but will grow in partial shade. It blooms April to June in warm deserts and June to July in cool mountain areas, and can be cut back after first bloom to encourage a second show in autumn. For a colorful, easy-care ground cover, rockrose should be spaced 2' to 3' apart.

Rockrose avoids drought with its deep roots—soak it occasionally to promote vigorous growth and heavy bloom. Plant rockrose in rock gardens, in containers, with other dry-loving perennials, or as a neat dry-garden edging. With poor drainage, rockrose may succumb to root rot. Like all evergreens, this plant benefits from a protective covering in cold, dry winters. Drape it with cut juniper boughs in autumn, and be sure to remove the boughs early in spring.

'Single Yellow' rockrose has bright yellow flowers and green leaves (6" high by 18" wide). 'Rose Glory' has a spreading growth habit, glossy green foliage, and a month-long display of bright rose-pink flowers (3" high by 18" wide).

Potential problems: be careful not to overwater young plants—check for soil moisture with a moisture meter and, after two weeks, water rockrose only when soil moisture registers as "low."

CORAL BELLS
Heuchera sanguinea
Category: shade (deserts), sun to partial shade (uplands and mountains)
Use: as border, in shade garden
Soil: any; does well in alkaline soils
Hardiness: all zones
Mature size: 12" to 18" high by 12" wide

Coral bells are small plants with rounded, dark green scallop-edged leaves 4" to 6" tall. Coral bells form neat evergreen mats in sun or shade. When in bloom (early summer and early fall), its deep pink to carmine red flowers are irresistible to hummingbirds and butterflies..

Coral bells need shade and regular water in deserts and warm inland areas. In cooler upland and mountain gardens, they grow and bloom in light conditions from full sun to shade. Coral bells will thrive in any soil as long as it is not soggy. In dry climates, weekly watering will promote good growth and vigorous bloom. Clumps spread slowly; once mature, they should be divided every three to four years to renew growth.

Coral bells are dazzling companions to perennial candytuft (*Iberis sempervirens*), golden columbine (*Aquilegia chrysantha*), sweet bedstraw (*Galium odoratum*), bellflower (*Campanula* species), and Autumn Joy sedum (*Sedum spectabile* 'Autumn Joy'). They make excellent container plants, small area ground cover, foundation plantings, low perennial borders, rock garden dwellers, and dry-shade inhabitants under oak trees. When interplanted with spring bulbs, their dark green leaves provide a strong contrast to hyacinths, freesias, Siberian squills (*Scilla* species), and daffodils (*Narcissus* species). 'Bressingham' hybrids are similar in size and culture. 'Bressingham White' has long-blooming white flowers; 'Firefly' blooms are bright red.

Potential problems: coral bells may be short-lived in hot desert gardens. Keep dust off leaves to prevent spider mites. In mild winter areas, check the undersides of leaves for mealybugs, slugs, and snails.

RED-HOT POKER
Kniphofia uvaria
Category: sun perennial
Use: in hummingbird garden
Soil: any; well-drained
Hardiness: zones 4 through 9
Mature size: 3' by 3'

Red-hot poker blossoms from the bottom to the top of tall flower spikes that take many days to completely unfold. It has spikes of tubular flowers that change color as they mature, flaming orange at the top and pale yellow at the bottom. Related to aloes and lilies, these stately plants have tall rosettes of bright green strap-like leaves and are attractive to hummingbirds.

Plant red-hot pokers in a sunny, well-drained spot. In mountain areas, they grow well in most years without being watered. In coldest areas, dried leaves left on the plant over winter will provide protection for developing flower buds—braid or tie them above clumps and secure with jute for a neat appearance.

The red flowers and green leaves of red-hot pokers look beautiful beside blue- and gray-leafed plants. To orchestrate a dramatic succession of bold bloom from spring to fall, plant red-hot pokers with oriental poppy (*Papaver orientale*), fragrant and Eaton's penstemons (*Penstemon palmeri* and *P. eatonii*), Russian sage (*Perovskia atriplicifolia*), blue sage (*Salvia azurea* var. *grandiflora*), and New Mexico sunflowers (*Helianthus maximilianii*).

Red-hot pokers vary in their cold tolerance—in areas of extreme cold, ask neighbors for offsets from established clumps. Newer forms include dwarfs (1½' high) to giants (6' high) and coral, red, orange, peach, yellow, near-white, and light-green flower colors. The 5½' high by 3' wide blue-leaf red-hot poker (*Kniphofia caulescens*) provides a spectacular floral display (zones 5 to 9).

Potential problems: deer and rabbit resistant. Red-hot pokers do not do well in hot deserts, but aloes and hesperaloes will serve many of the same functions.

Red-hot poker (*Kniphofia uvaria*)

ABOVE: Showy four o'clock (*Mirabilis multiflora*)
BELOW: Mexican evening primrose (*Oenothera speciosa*)

SHOWY FOUR O'CLOCK
Mirabilis multiflora
Category: sun perennial
Use: in dry gardens
Soil: any; best in lean-mineral soils
Hardiness: zones 4 to 10; treat as an annual in cold climates
Mature size: 18" by 3'

Showy four o'clock is a wonderful, gray-leafed mounding perennial, with a long succession of showy tubular magenta flowers that open in the afternoon and stay open all night. Flowers last only one evening, fading by midmorning, but are replaced anew each afternoon.

Because it stores water in a large tuberous root, showy four o'clock looks well-tended in dry gardens and blooms abundantly with summer heat. Native to dry plant communities of Arizona, New Mexico, southern Colorado, and Texas, showy four o'clock does well in nearly any soil. Mature plants require only occasional deep watering to look their best. Plant showy four o'clock in full sun or at the dripline of native trees and shrubs in hot summer locations.

Wild four o'clocks are great in combination with native cacti, hummingbird trumpets (*Zauschneria* species), globe mallows (*Sphaeralcea* species), evening primroses (*Oenothera* species), and shrubby Cleveland, rose, purple, and white sages (*Salvia clevelandii, S. pachyphylla, S. dorrii,* and *S. apiana*). Their neat mounding form goes well in the foreground of cacti and succulents, including prickly beavertails (*Opuntia basilaris*), purple prickly pears (*O. santa-rita*), desert prickly pears (*O. engelmannii* and *O. phaeacantha*), and yuccas (*Yucca* species). They also provide outstanding summer color accent in mass plantings of native grasses.

Another garden favorite, the 'Marvel of Peru' (*Mirabilis jalapa*), is an upright perennial with hundreds of white, red, pink, yellow, or marbled pink and white flat-faced flowers on 3' high and 3' wide bright green branching stems with long oval leaves.

Potential problems: requires very little care; when planting, be sure to keep the top of the tuberous root just above soil level.

MEXICAN EVENING PRIMROSE
Oenothera speciosa
Category: sun perennial
Use: in dry garden, as ground cover
Soil: any; best in lean-mineral soils
Hardiness: zones 5 to 11
Mature size: 10" by 18"

With large, four-petaled rose-pink flowers blooming throughout summer, Mexican evening primrose is a delicate-looking perennial that can take the heat and sun. It spreads rapidly by underground runners. Once it is established, only infrequent watering is needed. Mexican evening primrose makes a good ground cover or mass planting wherever its aggressive growth is an asset. It is just the plant for southern- and western-facing slopes.

Plant Mexican evening primrose in drifts amid masses of drought-loving perennials such as Russian sage (*Perovskia atriplicifolia*), giant catmint (*Nepeta* x 'Six Hills Giant'), Jerusalem sage (*Phlomis fruticosa*), trailing rosemary (*Rosmarinus officinalis* 'Prostrata'), and 'Sunray' coreopsis.

Members of the evening primrose family include:

Ozark sundrops (*Oenothera missouriensis*)—this low-growing plant (9" high by 2' wide); hardy in all zones, has bright green leaves and a constant supply of showy 4" yellow flowers;

Sundrops (*Calylophus* species)—these 9" high by 2' wide plants, hardy in all zones, form neat green mounds covered with yellow flowers. The flowers of Fendler's sundrops (*Calylophus hartwegii* var. *fendleri*) dry to red orange, giving a particularly sunny cast to this drought-loving perennial;

Tufted evening primrose (*Oenothera caespitosa*)—this 6" to 12" high by 1' to 3' wide low water–use beauty, hardy in all zones, has gray leaves and 4" white flowers;

'Whirling butterflies' (*Gaura lindheimeri*)—the countless ½" snowy white flowers on this 4' high by 3' wide graceful garden favorite, hardy in zones 5 to 11, evoke a migration of butterflies that have come down to sun themselves on its upright stems.

Potential problems: be sure not to plant it near less competitive plants; it will take over. If plants become rangy, cut back after bloom.

EATON'S FIRECRACKER
Penstemon eatonii
Category: sun perennial
Use: as border; in rock gardens, dry gardens, and containers
Soil: dry, well-drained
Hardiness: zones 5 to 11
Mature size: 3' high by 2' wide

Eaton's firecracker, a penstemon, is a prolific wildflower with majestic, 3' tall flower stalks of fire-engine red, long tubular flowers. This dry-loving perennial has a basal cluster of shiny dark green leaves. It can be planted in a dry border, against a hot wall, on a rocky slope, or any place where sun and good drainage prevail. It makes a striking containerized accent plant near patios, entries, pools, and water features.

Plant Eaton's firecracker high with the crown just above soil level. In low deserts, Eaton's firecracker can be grown with full sun, morning sun, or light shade; everywhere else it needs full sun. Penstemons love sun and lean, well-drained soils. Flowers are red, blue, purple, pink, and occasionally white. You can enjoy season-long penstemon bloom in the garden by planting several varieties with a succession of bloom times:

Parry's penstemon (*Penstemon parryi*)—tall flower stems with hot pink to rose-colored tubular flowers above gray leaves (zones 5 to 11).

Pine-leaf penstemon (*Penstemon pinifolius*)—neat, shrubby 1' tall evergreen with bright green needle-like leaves and a rich covering of tubular red flowers. Yellow ('Mersea Yellow') and orange ('Shades of Mango') flower forms are available, as are named varieties of trailing and compact forms. This is an excellent, low-maintenance plant hardy in all zones, but protect it from hot sun in deserts.

Rocky Mountain penstemon (*Penstemon strictus*)—bright purple flowers on 2½' tall stems above a 6" mat of medium-textured green leaves (zones 3 to 8).

Potential problems: once established, infrequent deep watering will keep plants vigorous and in heavy bloom.

Eaton's firecracker (*Penstemon eatonii*)

RUSSIAN SAGE
Perovskia atriplicifolia
Category: sun perennial
Use: as background, tall border
Soil: any; well-drained, fertile
Hardiness: all zones
Mature size: 4' tall by 3' to 4' wide

Russian sage is a silvery-leafed xeric subshrub (a perennial plant that becomes woody only at the base), covered with furry lavender and purple tubular blooms. When Russian sage is not blooming, its airy gray foliage softens the appearance of rocks and counteracts the glare in dry gardens. Russian sage grows in any soil, doing best in well-drained, open, fertile soil. Hardy in all zones, it subsists on natural water at high elevations; in deserts, it needs semiweekly to weekly water.

Be sure to space plants at least 4' apart so that they can develop their full stature and intricate branching form. If space is tight, try 'Filigran', a selection with small stature and finely dissected leaves. To promote healthy growth, Russian sage should be pruned to a height of 6" to 12" after it blooms. The sweet-scented flowers attract butterflies and bees.

The flowers of pink evening primrose (*Oenothera speciosa* 'Rosea'), fragrant penstemon (*Penstemon palmeri*), 'Cherry Red' autumn sage (*Salvia greggii* 'Cherry Red'), orange butterfly-weed (*Asclepias tuberosa*), and red bird-of-paradise (*Caesalpinia pulcherrima*) all look brighter in the presence of Russian sage.

When choosing companion plants, stick with easy-care plants with similar water needs and you will be rewarded with a guaranteed beautiful garden! One simple planting consists of a solitary Russian sage planted behind three rose-purple tall phlox (*Phlox paniculata*), one gloriosa daisy (*Rudbeckia hirta*), and a mound of 'Coronation Gold' yarrow (*Achillea filipendulina* 'Coronation Gold'). Another effective garden grouping includes yellow-flowered brittlebush, Parry's penstemon, and a low edging of 'Blue Wonder' catmint with a backdrop of Russian sage.

Potential problems: deer and rabbits avoid this plant's pungent foliage.

GLORIOSA DAISY
Rudbeckia hirta
Category: sun perennial
Use: as background, tall border
Soil: any
Hardiness: zones 4 to 11
Mature size: 3' to 4' tall by 3' to 4' wide

Gloriosa daisies are one of the wonders of the wildflower world—admired in nature, then cultivated to bring awe-inspiring beauty to the home garden. Flowerheads are 5" to 7" across and have broad golden yellow petals banded with orange, bronze, and mahogany arranged in radiant symmetry around fuzzy, dark brown central cones.

ABOVE: Russian sage (*Perovskia atriplicifolia***)**
BELOW: Gloriosa daisy (*Rudbeckia hirta***)**

Amaranth (*Amaranthus* species)

At peak bloom, flowers virtually cover all the leaves. These summer-blooming perennials are short-lived, but always put on a spectacular show. They are likely to bloom the first year, even when planted from seed sown in early spring. They make fabulous cut flowers, singly or in a mixed bouquet. Try several in a cobalt blue vase.

Gloriosa daisies can be planted singly, as foundation plantings along masonry walls, or in pots and planters. My favorite Gloriosa daisy variety is 'Pinwheel', with its mahogany and gold flowers. For small gardens and low borders, try 'Goldilocks' (to 18" high). Gloriosa daisies are long-blooming and their individual flowers are long-lasting. They often bloom into the fall, when few other species are looking their best.

Coneflowers are nearly always covered with butterflies or bees! Two related species are:

Cut-leaf coneflower (*Rudbeckia laciniata*)—a 6' tall by 3' wide perennial butterfly-magnet, hardy in all zones, with 4" diameter bright yellow coneflowers and large bright green leaves;

'Golden Glow' coneflower (*Rudbeckia laciniata* 'Golden Glow')—a 6' to 7' tall plant hardy in all zones, with golden yellow double blooms summer through fall.

Potential problems: they require regular watering and grow best with heat.

ANNUALS

RED AMARANTH
Amaranthus cruentus
Category: sun annual
Use: as background, filler, color accent
Soil: any; best in dry or well-drained
Hardiness: zones 4 to 11
Mature size: 5' high by 3' wide

Red amaranth's leaves, stems, and flowers all are red. Amaranths produce edible seeds that are a sure bet to bring birds to your garden. Plant red amaranth with similar large-stature and coarse-textured plants, including Rocky Mountain bee plant (*Cleome serrulata*) and Prince's plume (*Stanleya pinnata*). In small gardens, one plant can serve as an accent or focal point. Massed, amaranths create an effective screen. An informal amaranth hedge at the edge of a vegetable garden forms a beautiful backdrop for the contrasting colors of corn, sunflower, scarlet runner bean, dill, bronze fennel, and golden lemon thyme.

Plant amaranth in a sunny location or in partial or morning sun in hot desert gardens. Plants are grown from seed sown in fall in warmer temperature zones and in spring after the danger of last frost in all climate zones. At the end of the growing season, cut plants to the ground or leave dried stems in place to feed birds.

Other amaranths to consider are:

Cockscombs (*Celosia* species)—related plants of small stature. Plant dwarf forms (10" to

Cosmos (*Cosmos bipinnatus*)

12" tall) in smaller garden spaces or in a low border in front of a bed of red amaranth;

Joseph's coat (*Amaranthus tricolor*)—a 1' to 3' high by 2' wide upright branching plant grown for its many-colored leaves with patches of green, white, and red;

Love lies bleeding (*Amaranthus caudatus*)—a 3' high by 3' wide green-leafed sprawling plant with red flowers in very long pendant tassels.

Potential problems: seeds need to be watered daily until established; then, reduce watering to once weekly.

COSMOS
Cosmos bipinnatus
Category: sun annual
Use: for mass planting, background, border, filler, cut flowers, or in butterfly garden
Soil: any; not compacted
Hardiness: all zones
Mature size: 2' to 6' tall by 1' to 3' wide

Given ample sun, regular water, and open, prepared soils, cosmos rewards the gardener with quick growth, vibrant green leaves, and large daisy-type flowers. The blooms' bright yellow centers and petals in shades of white, pink, lavender, and purple are favored butterfly perches.

Cosmos are summer bloomers, best grown from seed planted in fall in warm deserts and after the last frost in cooler or upland areas. Just before seeding, loosen soil with a fork to a depth of at least 8" and incorporate a light dusting of 1" to 2" of compost or composted manure. Next, broadcast seed and rake in lightly. You can also seed cosmos directly into large containers.

If you left the packet of seed unplanted on the garage bench, take heart. Most nurseries stock plants in sizes from starts to gallon containers throughout the growing season. Water these thoroughly until established. Cosmos are best in mass plantings, in borders, and in backgrounds. They combine well with other tall flowering plants like cut-leaf coneflowers (*Rudbeckia laciniata*), whirling butterflies (*Gaura lindheimeri* 'Siskyou Pink'), and calliopsis (*Coreopsis tinctoria*).

Many varieties of cosmos are chosen for their compact growth, unusual flower color (yellow, orange, multicolored, or striped petals), or flower form (double, crested, or frilled). Compact varieties do well in containers and in formal garden locations. *Cosmos sulphureus* (yellow cosmos) has yellow flowers. Chocolate cosmos (*Cosmos atrosanguineus*) is a perennial with deep red, nearly brown, chocolate-scented flowers.

Potential problems: cosmos is not particular about soil, but responds with dramatic growth to soil that is fertile; allowed to set seed, it will self-sow.

ABOVE: Common sunflower (*Helianthus annuus*)
BELOW: Mullein pink (*Lychnis coronaria*)

COMMON SUNFLOWER
Helianthus annuus
Category: sun annual
Use: for mass planting, background, border, cut flowers, butterflies and birds, edible seeds
Soil: any; very tolerant of alkaline soil
Hardiness: all zones
Mature size: depends on variety

Summer sunflowers shoot upward to produce large flowers with yellow disks and petals of golden yellow, white, burgundy, russet, and near brown. Sunflowers also usher autumn into the garden. 'Mammoth Russian', perhaps the most loved variety, sports one enormous flower head on a single 6' to 10' tall stem.

Because sunflowers face toward the sun and track its course across the sky, plant them where they can be viewed from the east, south, and west. Sow seed directly into tilled ground about ½" deep in spring, cover, and firm soil. If you'd like to enjoy nonstop sunflowers, plant a new crop of seeds every two weeks. If you want to eat the seeds, cover young flower heads with netting; later collect mature heads and place them in paper bags in a dry, shady location until the seeds dry.

My sunflower favorite varieties are: 'Indian Blanket'—red with yellow tips to 4' to 5' tall; 'Italian White'—creamy ivory to 5' tall; 'Moonshadow'—pale yellow to 4' tall; 'Prado Red'—deep cranberry red to 4' tall; 'Velvet Queen'—multicolored fall shades of bronze, claret, and mahogany to 6' tall.

For smaller gardens and low borders, try 'Teddy Bear', with huge double-petaled golden pompoms over a compact green plant only 1½' tall.

Maximillian's sunflower (*Helianthus maximilianii*) is an autumn-blooming perennial hardy in all zones. Each of its 3' to 10' high green leafy stems is topped with a ladder of 2" yellow flowers from late summer into fall.

Potential problems: sunflowers need regular water and fertile soil.

MULLEIN PINK
Lychnis coronaria
Category: sun annual
Use: as filler, color accent, in butterfly garden
Soil: any; dry or well-drained
Hardiness: all zones
Mature size: 2' high by 3' wide

Mullein pink is an easy-to-grow annual with a long blooming period. Brilliant 1" magenta flowers top furry white stems and leaves from spring to early summer. Mullein pink needs morning or full-day sun and little water once established. It will naturalize and attract hummingbirds and butterflies.

Best used massed or in informal borders, mullein pink's white foliage contrasts nicely with equally nonthirsty green-leafed perennials like autumn sage (*Salvia greggii*) and chuparosa

(*Justicia californica*). Its shockingly vibrant flower colors complement bright yellow desert marigolds (*Baileya multiradiata*), wine cups (*Callirhoe involucrata*), and pink-flowered penstemons (try 'Sunset Crater' penstemon [*Penstemon clutei*] in mountain gardens, fragrant penstemon [*Penstemon palmeri*] at mid-elevations, and Parry's penstemon [*Penstemon parryi*] in warm desert gardens). Try it as a background plant for lamb's ears (*Stachys byzantina*), cottage pinks, and marigolds.

Mullein pink is related to carnations and pinks (*Dianthus* species) and catchflys (*Silene* species). Hummingbirds love Maltese cross (*Lychnis chalcedonica*), an outstanding 2' to 4' clumping mullein pink relative that is hardy in all zones and needs moderate moisture and full sun to partial shade. This summer-blooming perennial has bright green leaves and upright stems that end in dense terminal clusters of bright red five-petaled flowers. Give Maltese cross an eastern or northern exposure, regular water, and a protected location in hot desert areas.

Potential problems: this plant has few problems and tolerates difficult conditions, including drought, bright sun, and drying winds. Overwatering in heavy soils will cause leaves and stems to flop and yellow. Mullein pink self-sows freely; if you want to prevent this, remove seed capsules before they open.

GROUND COVERS

WINE CUPS
Callirhoe involucrata
Category: sun perennial
Use: in butterfly gardens
Soil: any; dry or well-drained
Hardiness: all zones
Mature size: 6" high by 2' to 3' wide

Wine cups hail from the Great Plains and Texas and do best in coarse-textured mineral soils. Bright sun is necessary to bring them into full bloom, when they are covered with large five-petaled, goblet-shaped magenta and white flowers on upright stems above five-lobed leathery dark green leaves.

Plant wine cups as a ground cover near Mexican evening primrose (*Oenothera speciosa*), stemless evening primrose (*Oenothera caespitosa*), Angelita daisy (*Hymenoxys acaulis*), California poppy (*Eschscholzia californica*), Fendler's sundrop (*Calylophus fendleri*), and trailing lantana (*Lantana montevidensis*); or between drifts of blue sage (*Salvia azurea*), Colorado blue spruce (*Picea pungens*), chamisa (*Chrysothamnus nauseosus*), coneflower (*Echinacea purpurea*), sand sage (*Artemisia filifolia*), or 'Autumn Joy' sedum (*Sedum spectabile* 'Autumn Joy'). For a low-water, low-care parkway strip, mix wine cups with hollyhocks (*Althea rosea*) and desert mallow (*Sphaeralcea ambigua*).

Wine cups (*Callirhoe involucrata*)

Wine cups require little maintenance. In desert zones, they need weekly water and an organic mulch to cool their roots. At high elevations, water wine cups infrequently and provide a rock mulch to keep roots warm. Plant 3" pots from early spring to midsummer in low elevation zones and in summer to fall in high elevations. Seed can be sown outdoors in fall, but germination is not always reliable. Before planting, loosen soil to a depth of 6" to 12" to encourage water penetration and fast growth of the large, fleshy roots. A related species, white-flowered poppy mallow (*Callirhoe alceoides*), has similar uses and needs.

Potential problems: wine cups tolerate many difficult conditions, but must have good drainage. In heavy soils, prevent crown rot by planting wine cups high on slopes or mounds. Be sure to plant with the crown just above soil level.

TRAILING LANTANA
Lantana montevidensis
Category: sun perennial
Use: as border
Soil: any
Hardiness: zones 9 to 11
Mature size: 1' to 2' high by 2' to 6' wide

Trailing lantana loves reflected sun and intense heat. It forms a dense, spreading green mat, nearly covered with large domes of yellow-eyed lavender to violet flowers that make it a favorite of butterflies from summer to fall. Trailing lantana blooms concurrently with red and yellow birds-of-paradise (*Caesalpinia pulcherrima* and *Caesalpinia gilliesii*), oleander (*Nerium oleander*), and moss verbena (*Verbena pulchella*). It provides a unifying filler between desert trees and shrubs, and its quick growth and heavy bloom make it a great choice for hanging baskets and container gardens.

In winter, trailing lantana becomes a bit scraggly; heavy pruning in early spring stimulates dense new growth. At low elevations, plant trailing lantana in spring. At higher elevations, treat trailing lantana as an annual, planting only after all danger of frost is past. Or keep it in a container and move it into a sunroom for winter. At high elevations, trailing lantana combines beautifully with 'Butterfly Blue' and 'Pink Mist' pincushion flower (*Scabiosa*), blue sage (*Salvia azurea* var. *grandiflora*), and butterfly weed (*Asclepias tuberosa*).

Upright shrubby lantana (*Lantana camara*), which grows to 3' to 6' high by 3' to 6' wide, tolerates slightly more frost. *L. camara* 'Radiation' bears red and orange flowers, and 'Snow White' has white flowers with yellow eyes. Hybrids between trailing and shrubby lantana have flowers of white, bicolor purple and pink, orange, yellow, or gold.

Potential problems: trailing lantana tolerates filtered light or morning sun; but too much shade, water, or fertilizer results in leggy growth and reduced bloom. Make sure to water deeply and infrequently. Yellow leaves are a sign of overwatering. Lantana has few pests, but may attract whiteflies.

Orange and red lantana (*Lantana* hybrid)

STAR JASMINE
Trachelospermum jasminoides
Category: partial shade shrub or vine
Use: for fragrance
Soil: any
Hardiness: zones 9 to 10
Mature size: 1½' to 2' high by 4' to 5' wide

Glossy dark green leaves and intensely fragrant star-shaped flowers make star jasmine one of the Southwest's most popular ground covers. Star jasmine is always neat and well-behaved. New growth is light green; leaves may turn bronze-red with winter chill.

Plant star jasmine in morning sun or shade in hot deserts, full sun in cooler areas. Star jasmine can be planted in spring or fall and grows well under trees like velvet mesquite (*Prosopis velutina*) and desert willow (*Chilopsis linearis*) that receive regular watering. To quickly form a dense ground cover, place plants 1½' to 2' apart; pinch branch tips, making sure to cut the dominant upright branch. Unless pinched, star jasmine will grow as a vine to 20' tall. Water regularly throughout summer and sparingly in winter. Give star jasmine a balanced fertilizer in spring and at the end of summer once heat begins to subside.

Star jasmine can be treated as a fragrant annual or container plant for full sun in zones 4 to 8. When perennial plants are needed for similar landscape uses in colder zones 4 to 8, substitute creeping Oregon grape (*Mahonia repens*) or low-growing manzanitas (*Arctostaphylos* species) such as kinnikinnick (*Arctostaphylos uva-ursi*), pine-mat manzanita (*Arctostaphylos nevadensis*), and Colorado manzanita (*Arctostaphylos uva-ursi* x *nevadensis*).

Potential problems: spray leaves with water during periods of low humidity to prevent spider mites, and watch for scale insects on the bottom of leaves and on stems.

MOSS VERBENA
Verbena pulchella
Category: sun or light shade perennial
Use: in butterfly gardens
Soil: any; dry, well-drained
Hardiness: zones 9 to 10
Mature size: 1' high by 2' to 3' wide

This fast-growing ground cover is covered with showy clusters of rose violet five-petaled flowers from spring to fall. Like all verbenas, it is an excellent butterfly plant.

Planted in mass with wildflowers, moss verbena makes an attractive blooming filler and is effective for erosion control. Highly adapted to desert conditions, it needs hot sun, reflected heat, and only infrequent water. Both growth and blooming slow at the height of summer heat and when temperatures dip below freezing. Plant it with other dry-loving species, including Cleveland sage (*Salvia clevelandii*), Mexican sage (*Salvia leucantha*), and autumn sage (*Salvia greggii*), or between cacti, desert trees, and succulents.

ABOVE: Star jasmine (*Trachelospermum jasminoides*)
BELOW: Moss Verbena (*Verbena pulchella*)

Creeping Oregon grape (*Mahonia repens*)

They make excellent container plants and small area ground covers.

Related species include:

Dakota verbena (*Verbena bipinnatifida*)—a 1½' high by 2' wide sprawling perennial, hardy in all zones, with large clusters of fragrant red-violet flowers;

New Mexico verbena (*Verbena macdougalii*)— a 3' tall perennial hardy in zones 3 to 8 with lavender flowers on upright, candelabra-like spikes;

Gooding's verbena (*Verbena goodingii*)—a low-growing 6" to 9" high by 3' wide perennial with lavender flowers, hardy in zones 6 to 11;

Peruvian verbena (*Verbena peruviana*)—forms a 3" high by 3' wide dark-green mat topped with clusters of scarlet and white flowers;

Sandpaper verbena (*Verbena rigida*)—an upright perennial hardy in all zones with purple flowers to 3' tall; blooms the first summer from spring-planted seed.

Potential problems: verbenas have few pests or problems, but need good drainage.

CREEPING OREGON GRAPE
Mahonia repens
Category: shade to sun shrub
Use: for naturalizing cover
Soil: any
Hardiness: all zones
Mature size: 1' to 3' tall spreading

Creeping Oregon grape forms a dense ground cover that tolerates heavy soils and checks soil erosion. In spring, its clear yellow flowers burst forth in large rounded clusters, while new leaves emerge in shades of bronze, lime, and pink. In summer, bountiful bunches of blue-black berries, which bring birds to the garden, can be gathered to make jelly. In fall, its shiny leaves are variegated with forest green, deep red, and purple. Year round, this western native clothes the ground with a dense, low cover of leathery holly-like leaves, and is drought-tolerant.

It grows in all light conditions, but needs regular water with heat and sun. Cut creeping Oregon grape to the ground in spring to rejuvenate leaves and maintain a compact growth habit; it can be mowed periodically at a blade height of 4". In shady gardens, plant creeping Oregon grape with heavenly bamboo to create a lush garden with low water use.

Creeping Oregon grape is related to many effective barrier plants. Oregon grape (*Mahonia aquifolium*) is hardy in all zones and has a 6' high upright growth habit, shiny green leaves, and the same flower and fruiting characteristics as its creeping cousin. Cultivar 'Compacta' is 2' tall. Fremont barberry (*Mahonia fremontii*), red mahonia (*Mahonia haematocarpa*), and algerita (*Mahonia trifoliolata*) all have gray, holly-like leaves, yellow flowers, and bright red berries that attract birds and make tasty jellies. Fremont barberry is hardiest in zones 5 to 8. Red mahonia is intermediate in cold tolerance (zones 8 to 10). Algerita grows best in deserts (zones 9 to 11).

Potential problems: in hot deserts, it needs a protected, shady location and regular water.

ABOVE: Blue fescue (*Festuca glauca*)
BELOW: Little bluestem (*Schizachyrium scoparium*)

GRASSES

BLUE FESCUE
Festuca glauca
Category: sun to shade ornamental grass
Use: as edging, filler, in small areas
Soil: any; best in dry
Hardiness: all zones
Mature size: 6' to 12' high by 6" to 12" wide

This compact bunchgrass is planted for its easy care and beautiful blue-gray leaves. It makes a ground cover that withstands occasional foot traffic. Try it with other ornamental grasses in front of a succulent border of purple prickly pear (*Opuntia santa-rita*), red hesperaloe (*Hesperaloe parviflora*), and yucca.

In summer, blue fescue displays upright flowering stalks of petal-less flowers several inches above its leaves; these cure to tan. Blue fescue's leaves contrast nicely with the red fall foliage of purple geranium (*Geranium caespitosum*), dragonsblood sedum (*Sedum spurium* 'Dragon's Blood'), and purple threeawn (*Aristida purpurea*). Blue fescue also makes a nice rock garden plant in dry shade.

Blue fescue is planted in spring and divided in fall. It requires frequent watering until established. Early-season grooming renews growth and increases vigor—cut established plants to a height of 3" or rake out thatch with a garden rake once yearly in spring.

In high elevations, try sheep fescue (*Festuca ovina*), a 1' tall clumping grass that is frequently seeded as a low water–use turf grass, and Arizona fescue (*Festuca arizonica*), a species that tolerates heavy soils.

Potential problems: no pests or diseases.

LITTLE BLUESTEM
Schizachyrium scoparium
Category: sun perennial grass
Use: for mass planting, slopes, informal borders, fall color
Soil: any; must be well-drained
Hardiness: zones 3 to 10
Mature size: 2' to 4' high by 2' wide

Little bluestem is a warm-season bunchgrass (its period of active growth takes place when temperatures are high, in contrast to "cool-season" grasses, which have their period of active growth during cool times of year). In summer it sends up flowering stems. In fall it comes into its full beauty as long-awned, zigzag seedheads fully ripen to fluffy white. With the first fall chill, bluestem's leaf blades change from green to shades of deep orange, red, or red-violet.

Little bluestem needs full sun and good drainage. It can be planted in mass, or in drifts with other dry-loving grasses, wildflowers, and succulents, including blue sage (*Salvia azurea*), purple prairie clover (*Petalostemon purpureum*), and trailing indigo bush (*Dalea greggii*). Its fall color contrasts beautifully with blue, gray, and silver foliage—try it with chamisa (*Chrysothamnus nauseosus*), Texas ranger (*Leucophyllum* species), or prairie sagebrush (*Artemisia ludoviciana*).

Little bluestem attracts birds and butterflies. It does best given an occasional deep watering during the summer months. Cut down old stems in early spring to keep it looking its best.

Several varieties of little bluestem are chosen for their leaf color and stupendous fall display. 'The Blues' has upright intensely blue foliage (to 3'), which turns burgundy-red in fall. 'Blaze' has a tight upright growth habit (2' high by 15" wide) and vivid red fall color.

Potential problems: no pests or diseases.

SHRUBS

CHUPAROSA
Justicia californica
Category: sun to light shade desert shrub
Use: in hummingbird gardens
Soil: any; well-drained
Hardiness: zone 10 and above
Mature size: 3' by 5'

Chuparosa is a critical nectar plant, sustaining hummingbirds throughout the winter with reliable bloom. Its tubular red flowers, gray-green rounded leaves, and intricate, open branching pattern also make it a must-have for desert home gardens.

Chuparosa has some flowers year round, with peak bloom from January to April and again from September to October. Plant chuparosa in fall or spring in any well-drained soil. Mature plants that die back to the ground with frost will resprout in the spring. Planting in areas with reflected heat (up against a wall, among boulders, or at the base of an existing tree) will speed establishment.

Chuparosa requires little effort to maintain. Its period of active growth is winter. Water only as necessary to prevent wilting and promote growth. Chuparosa is semideciduous and drops its leaves in extreme drought. In summer, you can keep plants leafy with an occasional deep soaking. Chuparosa is great in informal, natural gardens. It also makes a striking accent plant.

Potential problems: because it is slow to get started, buy large-sized plants; new starts need protection, particularly from rabbits and frost, until established.

Chuparosa (*Justicia californica*)

ABOVE: Autumn sage (*Salvia greggii*)
BELOW: Quail bush (*Atriplex lentiformis*)

AUTUMN SAGE
Salvia greggii
Category: sun-loving shrub
Use: for informal borders or mass planting
Soil: well-drained, fertile
Hardiness: zones 6 to 11
Mature size: 3' to 4' by 3' to 4'

Autumn sage blooms from fall to late spring in the desert and throughout summer in cooler zones in many shades of red, purple, yellow, white, and blue. Flowers are attractive to hummingbirds and butterflies.

The light green leaves of autumn sage turn bronze with winter chill. In hot deserts, give autumn sage light shade under the open canopy of trees like blue palo verde (*Cercidium floridum*) and desert willow (*Chilopsis linearis*). In the coldest zones, autumn sage freezes to the ground and resprouts in spring; plant with reflected heat and rock mulch and cover crowns with juniper boughs or pine needles for winter protection.

Mix autumn sage with lantana, chuparosa (*Justicia californica*), blue plumbago (*Ceratostigma plumbaginoides*), Texas ranger (*Leucophyllum frutescens*), purple prickly pear (*Opuntia santa-rita*), rosemary (*Rosmarinus officinalis*), and other sages, such as Mexican bush sage (*Salvia leucantha*) or pineapple sage (*S. elegans*).

Potential problems: mulch roots to keep soil from drying out; water once weekly in summer and less frequently year round. Cut back woody stems annually to renew growth.

QUAIL BUSH
Atriplex lentiformis
Category: sun-loving shrub
Use: for screens, mass planting, color accent, erosion control
Soil: any; will thrive in saline soils
Hardiness: zones 6 to 11
Mature size: 3' to 10' high by 6' to 12' wide

Attractive to quail and other birds, quail bush is the best saltbush for low and hot deserts. It is a densely branched, spreading large shrub with oval blue-gray leaves and clusters of golden seeds, planted for its foliage color, fast growth, and high wildlife value. Quail bush tolerates salty and alkaline soils, and endures intense heat and drought. Because it grows quickly under difficult desert conditions, it can be planted to form a quickly growing screen. If the shrubs outgrow their garden space, they can be severely cut back or pruned to desired shape.

The gray leaves and golden seeds of quail bush contrast nicely with green-leafed trees, shrubs, and perennials. In low deserts, pink flowering bougainvilleas and oleanders make attractive landscape companions. Both saltbush and quail bush can extract salt from saline soils and irrigation water and emit it through their leaves. For speedy growth, water quail bush deeply and regularly only during dry months. Their extensive root systems and quick above-ground growth make them excellent erosion-control plants on slopes, road cuts, and disturbed areas.

Four-wing salt bush (*Atriplex canescens*), hardy in all zones, is a smaller 4' high by 6' to 8' wide shrub with narrow silver leaves. In cold areas, it provides a good windbreak.

Potential problems: needs no fertilizer and requires little maintenance; very fire-resistant.

BUTTERFLY BUSH
Buddleia davidii
Category: sun-loving shrub or small tree
Use: for screens, mass planting, color accent, butterfly gardens
Soil: good drainage
Hardiness: zones 5 to 11
Mature size: 3' to 10' high by 5' to 15' feet wide

Butterfly bush is a fast-growing shrub with 12" long lilac-like clusters of fragrant purple, lavender, or white flowers borne on the ends of arching stems. In cold areas, plant butterfly bush against a south-facing wall with rocks and boulders for reflected heat. Deadhead regularly to prolong bloom and attract butterflies, including swallowtails, painted ladies, monarchs, and western checkerspots.

Butterfly bush can be evergreen or deciduous. In frost-free areas, it is a 10' tall evergreen; with extreme cold, its branches die back to the ground and new stems appear in spring. Butterfly bush blooms on the current season's growth. Except in cold zones, the best time to prune is just before spring growth begins. In cold areas, cut back severely in fall and mulch heavily.

Named varieties of butterfly bush include 'White Profusion' with 16" white flower clusters; 'Dark Knight' with dark purple-blue flowers; 'Harlequin' with thick panicles of dark red-violet flowers and green leaves with yellow margins; 'Royal Red', which attracts both butterflies and hummingbirds; and 3' to 5' tall dwarf butterfly bush (*Buddleia davidii nanhoensis*).

Other butterfly bushes include:

Fountain butterfly bush (*Buddleia alternifolia*), a 12' x 12' weeping tree hardy in zones 6 to 9 with gray leaves and fragrant purple flower clusters. It blooms on the previous year's growth;

Woolly butterfly bush (*Buddleia marrubiifolia*), a mid-sized 3' to 5' high by 4 to 5' wide shrub hardy in zones 7 to 11 with whorled bright orange flowers and fuzzy white leaves and stems.

Potential problems: requires good drainage, moist soil, and heat for blooming.

Butterfly bush (*Buddleia davidii*)

ABOVE: Red bird-of-paradise (*Caesalpinia pulcherrima*)
BELOW: Baja fairy duster (*Calliandra californica*)

RED BIRD-OF-PARADISE
Caesalpinia pulcherrima
Category: sun-loving shrub
Use: for mass planting, color accent, summer bloom
Soil: any; well-drained
Hardiness: zones 9 to 11
Mature size: 10' high by 6' to 12' wide

Red bird-of-paradise produces extravagant triangular clusters of deep red-orange and yellow ruffled flowers throughout the blistering hot months of summer. Its open flower arrangement and feathery light green leaves give this sparsely branched upright shrub a wispy look. But its delicate looks are deceiving—this plant is so tough it is planted in freeway medians in southern Arizona. Red bird-of-paradise is an important nectar plant for hummingbirds.

Red bird-of-paradise is impressive by itself or when planted in mass with trailing lantana (*Lantana montevidensis*), white flowering oleander, and moss verbena (*Verbena pulchella*). It makes an excellent container plant—in cold zones bring it indoors before the first frost. Cut plants back and apply organic fertilizer in spring. Water weekly throughout summer. Removing old flower clusters encourages more bloom. Plant red bird-of-paradise only in well-draining soils.

Yellow bird-of-paradise (*Caesalpinia gilliesii*) grows 5' to 10' high by 3 to 8' wide and has upright clusters of 1½" yellow flowers with bunches of showy long scarlet stamens. Hardy in zones 9 to 11, it can be trained as a single-trunk tree.

Cascalote (*Caesalpinia cacalaco*) is a 20' high by 15' wide winter-flowering tree with thorny branches and very showy, large yellow flowers. Hardy in zones 9 to 11, cascalote can be planted in full sun in sheltered locations to provide winter nectar for hummers.

Potential problems: heavy litter from flower and leaf drop can be messy—place plants away from pavement and swimming pools,where they create extra cleanup chores and clog pool filters.

BAJA FAIRY DUSTER
Calliandra californica
Category: sun-loving shrub
Use: for mass planting, edging, or informal hedges
Soil: any; well-drained
Hardiness: zones 9 to 11
Mature size: 4' to 5' by 4' to 5'

Baja fairy duster is an open shrub of medium height that draws in hummingbirds nonstop. Like mimosas, acacias, and bottlebrushes, Baja fairy duster belongs to the part of the pea family with petal-less flowers. Each blossom consists of dozens of bright red narrow stamens; several of these flowers group together to form scarlet puffball-type flowers. The red flowers and stems covered with dark green divided leaves are nicely offset by golden barrel cactus (*Echinocactus grusonii*), teddy bear and silver cholla (*Opuntia* spp.), golden-flowered and Parry's agave (*Agave chrysantha* and *Agave parryi*), brittlebush (*Encelia farinosa*), and Engelmann prickly pear (*Opuntia engelmannii*).

Bring on the sun and heat—this evergreen western native shrub needs both, along with good drainage. Water every other week in summer and frequently in winter if rains are sparse. Regular water encourages continuous bloom. If plants become leggy, cut them back to 1' in spring.

Fairy duster (*Calliandra eriophylla*) is a delicate-looking, drought-tolerant southwestern native shrub, hardy in zones 8 to 11, with spherical clusters of soft pink flowers. It grows to 3' to 4' by 4', blooms in winter, spring, and fall, and will remain evergreen and bloom longer when given water every two to three weeks in summer.

Potential problems: Baja fairy duster is self-mulching, dropping spent flowers and leaves on the ground. If you rake away this natural mulch, plan to provide plants with a 3" to 4" layer of organic mulch or composted manure to retain soil moisture and reduce irrigation needs.

APACHE PLUME
Fallugia paradoxa
Category: sun-loving shrub
Use: for mass planting, informal hedges
Soil: any; well-drained
Hardiness: zones 5 to 11
Mature size: 3' to 6' by 3' to 6'

Countless long-plumed white seeds that ripen to salmon pink in autumn are the showiest feature of this drought-tolerant southwestern native. Apache plume is a fine-textured gray-green shrub in the rose family. Its fragrant 1"-diameter, white five-petaled flowers with bright yellow centers look like miniature roses covering its pale branches in spring and summer. As flowers fade, they are replaced by seeds that remain on the plant throughout autumn and winter.

Apache plume takes full sun to partial shade and grows in a variety of conditions, from low deserts to dry, high-elevation pine and oak forests. At high elevations, it is often planted with native oak (*Quercus* species), chamisa (*Chrysothamnus nauseosus*), and manzanita (*Arctostaphylos* species) to create an easy-care shrub landscape. At lower elevations, it grows well with cacti, succulents, sages, and bright-flowered perennials. Try planting Apache plume, little bluestem (*Schizachyrium scoparium*), and pink muhly grass (*Muhlenbergia capillaris*) where they'll glow in the afternoon sun. Apache plume can be cut back heavily when young. It will resprout after fire or any disturbance. In deserts, it should be watered deeply every two weeks during summer for best growth and bloom.

Potential problems: does best in well-drained soils but can grow in clays as long as it is not overwatered.

Apache plume (*Fallugia paradoxa*)

HEAVENLY BAMBOO
Nandina domestica
Category: sun or shade shrub
Use: as hedge, screen, or container plant
Soil: any
Hardiness: zones 6 to 12
Mature size: 6' to 8' tall spreading

Heavenly bamboo's upright canes are covered with airy, intricately divided leaves. New foliage opens pink and bronze, turns next to bright green, darkens with maturity, and is tinged with purple, bronze, and red as fall turns into winter. Add 6" to 12" clusters of star-shaped light pink to creamy white flowers, which then turn into equally large bunches of shiny red berries. Plant some fragrant honeysuckle, jasmine, gardenias, or roses nearby, and your senses will be satiated.

Heavenly bamboo is not a true bamboo, but a barberry. It grows in sun or shade and develops its best leaf colors in full sun. It needs shade in hot desert areas and benefits from mulching. To speed its slow growth, plant it in rich soil and water regularly, or buy large plants for quick cover. Heavenly bamboo is evergreen in warm winter areas, but dies back to the ground in the coldest areas (then resprouts quickly in spring). In the coldest areas, plant heavenly bamboo in planters near sidewalks, boulders, or rocks for added root protection. Hedging, screening, filling narrow planting areas, and breaking up long sight lines are some of the best uses of heavenly bamboo. Plant in a large container for a moveable garden screen.

Keep heavenly bamboo at a height of 3' by removing the oldest canes at ground level; or purchase dwarf varieties—'Compacta' grows 4' to 5' tall and 'Woods Dwarf' has rounded form 3' to 4' tall, dense growth, and bright fall to winter foliage colors of crimson to scarlet. 'Nana' is a 1' to 3' tall mounding ground-cover form.

Potential problems: in alkaline soils, plants can become chlorotic.

OLEANDER
Nerium oleander
Category: sun-loving shrub
Use: as hedge, screen, or container plant
Soil: any; tolerates poor drainage and saline soil
Hardiness: zones 9 to 11
Mature size: varies; 3' to 30' by 3' to 12'

Oleander loves sun and reflected heat, grows in just about any soil, and is covered nearly year-round (May to October) with large bunches of fragrant five-petaled white, pink, salmon, yellow, red, or magenta flowers. It grows quickly and blooms heavily in the face of many difficult but common southwestern garden conditions—drought, heat, alkaline soils, sun, and wind.

Oleander needs bright sun to produce flowers. With shiny dark green leaves, it makes a great background, mass planting, or privacy screen, and is hassle-free and beautiful near swimming

ABOVE: Heavenly bamboo (*Nandina domestica*)
BELOW: Oleander (*Nerium oleander*)

Shrub cinquefoil (*Potentilla fruticosa* cultivar)

pools. If you'd like a flowering small tree for container or patio, oleander standards (trained with single trunks) are available.

The first consideration in oleander selection is mature size—there is a huge spread in height and width between varieties. Dwarfs can be kept between 3' to 4' tall, tall forms may top 20', and intermediate-height forms abound. Prune branch tips back slightly in spring to limit size and control form. (Wear gloves when pruning; the milky sap is irritating).

Oleander varieties differ in their cold tolerance. In zone 9, the hardiest oleanders die back to the ground and send up fast-growing shoots in the spring. Local nurseries and botanic gardens can clue you in on the best selection for your garden needs.

Potential problems: all parts of this plant are poisonous to people and pets. Deer will not eat oleander.

SHRUB CINQUEFOIL
Potentilla fruticosa
Category: sun to filtered light shrub
Use: as background, short hedge, container plant
Soil: any
Hardiness: all zones
Mature size: 3' to 4' by 3' to 4'

Sunny yellow open flowers dapple the surface of this neat, rounded gray-green shrub native to mountains throughout the northern hemisphere. In high-elevation gardens, the bloom is strongest and the form most compact in full sun. In hot-summer areas, shrub cinquefoil is best grown protected from afternoon sun and thrives with morning sun or filtered light. Peak bloom is June to October. Its flat flowers attract bees and butterflies.

Shrub cinquefoil needs regular water in summer, especially during dry periods in hot zones, but is surprisingly drought tolerant at elevations above 4,000'. A 3" deep layer of organic mulch laid out to its dripline will reduce water use. It makes a good short background plant in a border, an informal low hedge, or a neat easy-to-maintain large container plant. It thrives in rocky soils and can be planted on steep slopes for erosion control. In mountain gardens, shrub cinquefoil is frequently planted with quaking aspen trees and red-twig dogwood.

Drought tolerance varies among shrub cinquefoil. Cultivated varieties frequently require more water than western native strains. Varieties include: 'Abbotswood'—white blooms; 'Katherine Dykes'—with pale yellow, 1"-diameter flowers; 'Red Ace'—flowers open bright red with yellow underside and fade to yellow; 'Sutter's Gold'—clear yellow 1" flowers on a ground cover or edging shrub 1' high by 3' wide; 'Tangerine'—bright, yellow-orange flowers on 2½' shrub.

Potential problems: free of pests and diseases; requires only minimal pruning.

ABOVE: Three-leaf sumac (*Rhus trilobata*)
BELOW: Ocotillo (*Fouquieria splendens*)

THREE-LEAF SUMAC
Rhus trilobata
Category: sun to light shade shrub
Use: as background, informal hedge, for fall color
Soil: any; good drainage
Hardiness: all zones
Mature size: 8' by 8'

Three-leaf sumac is a deciduous shrub 8' tall and equally wide. Its three-lobed leaves erupt in shades of pink, bronze, and salmon; these age to a leathery green during summer, then turn to purple, red, and orange, creating a mound of glowing fall color. Flowers are inconspicuous. Its deep roots make it useful for erosion control; fruits and dense branches provide food and cover for birds and small mammals.

Once established, three-leaf sumac requires no supplemental water and responds with speedy growth to occasional deep irrigation. It resprouts after fire and can be cut to the ground in spring to reduce size and produce new shoots.

Useful sumac species include:

Evergreen sumac (*Rhus virens*)—a 12' by 12' evergreen native shrub with dark green leaves and red fruit that takes open shade and is hardy in zones 6 to 10;

'Gro-low' sumac (*Rhus aromatica* 'Gro-low')—a 2½' tall x 5' wide ground cover shrub, hardy in zones 4 to 9, with glossy green leaves turning red-orange in autumn;

Littleleaf sumac (*Rhus microphylla*)—an 8' high by 12' wide densely twiggy, low water user, hardy in zones 6 to 10, with small deciduous leaves and sticky red fruit, great for birds;

Smooth sumac (*Rhus glabra*)—a 10' to 20' spreading deciduous shrub or small tree, hardy in zones 4 to 9, with huge, divided leaves and intense red fall color;

Sugar bush (*Rhus ovata*)—an 8' by 8' rounded evergreen shrub, hardy in zones 7 to 11, with pink flower clusters and gray-green leaves.

Potential problems: does best in full sun at high elevations; in desert and interior areas, protect it from afternoon sun.

OCOTILLO
Fouquieria splendens
Category: sun shrub or multistem tree
Use: for mass planting, color accent
Soil: needs excellent drainage
Hardiness: zones 7 to 11
Mature size: 20' by 12'

Long an integral part of southwestern life, the ocotillo defies categorization. Succulent, shrub, or tree, the ocotillo is a plant of unusual form and unparalleled bloom.

Mature ocotillos consist of up to 25 tall, slender, thorny whip-like arching branches arising from the base. Small, rounded light green leaves sprout with moisture, are shed with water stress, and emerge again when water is plentiful. Long, crowded clusters of tubular, 1" long bright red flowers on branch tips erupt following spring rains and sometimes again after summer rains. Sweet-scented blossoms are like candy to hummingbirds; they are also pollinated by bats.

Ocotillos like a hot, well-drained location and can be grown at elevations to 5500'; they do especially well in sloping, rocky, or sandy soils. Ocotillos need water only once a month when they are actively growing. Their cold tolerance diminishes with excess water and fertilizer. Reduce irrigation as autumn approaches. In cold zones, plant them where they will receive protection from extremes of cold—on south-facing slopes, against warm walls, and surrounded with rocks.

For centuries, ocotillo canes have been planted to form living fences; to grow your own, cut branches and place them in the ground to root, being sure to water only occasionally until leaves sprout and stems begin to grow. Other uses include screens and barriers.

Potential problems: unless under stress (extremes of drought, too much water, or poor drainage), they are problem-free.

SUCCULENTS AND CACTI

RED HESPERALOE
Hesperaloe parviflora
Category: sun or shade succulent
Use: for accent, ground cover, container
Soil: any; well-drained
Hardiness: zones 5 to 11
Mature size: 3' to 5' by 3' to 6'

With its stellar performance in extremes of heat and cold, red hesperaloe is an ideal southwestern plant. Its many tall stems of long-lasting coral-red flowers arch up from a neat clump of narrow grass-like green leaves and attract hummingbirds and beneficial insects May to October.

Give red hesperaloe water every three weeks during summer and remove dead leaves; clumps spread slowly and can be divided in early spring. Hesperaloes do well in hot patio planters and large containers. Their upright flowers look great in mass plantings, either planted in informal curving swaths or in straight lines along paths and drives. One single clump makes a great accent plant in a small garden area.

Red flowers and green leaves are shown to their best advantage in beautiful combination with gray-leafed Artemisia; blue-gray chamisa; and yellow, red, and orange forms of pineleaf penstemon (*Penstemon pinifolius*). Red hesperaloe also combines well with cacti and succulents, particularly beargrass (*Nolina microcarpa*), desert spoon (*Dasylirion wheeleri*), and soaptree yucca (*Yucca elata*). At mid-elevations, try red hesperaloe with threadleaf-sagebrush (*Artemisia filifolia*) and prince's plume (*Stanley pinnata*). In high-elevation gardens, plant red hesperaloe in the foreground of fernbush (*Chamaebatiaria millefolium*), three-leaf sumac (*Rhus trilobata*), and silver buffaloberry (*Shepherdia argentea*).

Yellow forms of hesperaloe, hardy in zones 5 to 11, are smaller than red ones, with flower stalks to 4'. Night-flowering hesperaloe (*Hesperaloe nocturna*), hardy in zones 9 to 11, is 5' tall by 6' wide and has white flowers and a light fragrance that attracts hawk moths.

Potential problems: none.

Red Hesperaloe (*Hesperaloe parviflora*)

ABOVE: Santa Rita prickly pear (*Opuntia* santa-rita)
BELOW: Golden barrel cactus (*Echinocactus prusonii*)

SANTA RITA PRICKLY PEAR
Opuntia santa-rita
Category: cactus
Use: color accent, ground cover, informal hedge
Soil: any; well-drained
Hardiness: zones 8 to 11
Mature size: 6' x 6'

Both the soft, violet-tinged gray color and tree-like form of Santa Rita prickly pear make it a unique, desirable plant for dry gardens. Young pads are deep maroon. During winter chill and dry periods, the color of mature pads deepens to violet and may even become red. Large, lemon-yellow many-petaled flowers with bright red centers bloom along the top edges of pads in spring through summer. These are followed by spherical, spineless, purple-red fleshy fruits enjoyed by birds.

Santa Rita prickly pears sold in nurseries have few spines. They do well in large containers and sunny garden spots. To keep Santa Rita prickly pears looking their best, provide deep water no more than once a month in winter or twice a month in summer.

The genus Opuntia contains both prickly pears and chollas. Prickly pears have flat pads; chollas have cylindrical stems. Other Opuntias include:

Beavertail prickly pear (*Opuntia basilaris*)—2' high x 4' wide, with large velvety gray pads and magenta pink flowers, hardy in zones 6 to 11;

Desert Christmas cactus (*Opuntia leptocaulis*)—3' tall by 3' wide, with bright red fleshy fruits and dark green stems, hardy in zones 7 to 11;

Englemann prickly pear (*Opuntia engelmannii*)—5' tall by 15' wide, with yellow, orange, or reddish flowers, large edible pads (nopales), and fruits (las tunas), hardy in zones 4 to 11.

Potential problems: cacti may have spines, thorns, or irritating glochids.

GOLDEN BARREL CACTUS
Echinocactus grusonii
Category: cactus
Use: color accent
Soil: any; well-drained
Hardiness: zones 9 to 11
Mature size: 1' to 4' by 2' to 3'

Golden barrel cactus is a rounded, full-bodied cactus that glows with a network of spreading, stiff, bright yellow spines borne along sharply angled vertical ribs over its deep green surface. Shaped like an overstuffed hassock, this plant is also called mother-in-law's cushion. It makes a wonderful accent plant, can be planted singly or in groups, and bears bright yellow 1½" to 2½" flowers in summer.

Golden barrel cactus is a moderately slow grower; young plants are best placed where they will receive morning sun, partial shade, or filtered light. However, if you intend to put them in

Redbud (*Cercis* spp.)

a sunny location, they should be temporarily placed in a protected situation and only gradually moved out into full sun and planted. Plants are hardy to 20 degrees Fahrenheit. If you buy greenhouse-grown plants, acclimatize them to outdoor conditions gradually.

In cold climates, barrel cactus can be planted in large tubs or containers and brought indoors to a greenhouse or sunroom. Water established plants twice monthly in summer, every other month in winter. Plant golden barrel cactus with other desert plants with like water needs, including cacti—magenta-flowering Engelmann's hedgehog cactus (*Echinocereus engelmannii*) is an excellent addition to the visual feast—succulents, and drought-tolerant perennials. The golden glow and compact rounded form of this plant contrast beautifully with the long narrow blue-gray leaves of desert spoon (*Dasylirion wheeleri*) and American agave (*Agave americana*), the fan-shaped fronds of blue hesper palm (*Brahea armata*), and the purple flowers of ice plants.

Potential problems: overwatering; make sure soil or potting mixture is sharp and well drained to prevent root rot.

TREES

🌹

REDBUD
Cercis species
Category: tree
Use: for early bloom, fall color, shade
Soil: any; moist and well-drained
Hardiness: varies with species
Mature size: 10' to 25' by 10' to 25'

Redbuds are winter-deciduous small trees with stemless clusters of pink to magenta-red pea-like flowers. Their flowers bloom nonstop for two weeks. Then heart-shaped leaves unfurl, at first small and shiny bronze, next maturing to bright green, and finally turning yellow in fall. All redbuds provide cover, nest sites, and seeds for birds and are a source of early spring nectar for bees and butterflies.

Redbuds need regular water, particularly in the first two years after planting. After that, deep taproots make them moderately drought-tolerant. With good drainage, they can grow in any soil. Plant redbuds in full sun to dappled shade. To train redbuds to a single trunk tree, remove all suckers from the base in winter each year. Varieties include:

Chinese redbud (*Cercis chinensis*)—a densely branched 10' by 10' shrub; 'Avondale' is a compact selection with deep purple-pink flowers, hardy in zones 6 to 9;

Eastern redbud (*Cercis canadensis*)—grows to 30' by 30'; 'Alba' has white flowers and is hardy in zones 5 to 9;

Mexican redbud (*Cercis canadensis* var. *mexicana*)—this 25' by 25' tree gives afternoon shade in low desert. Hardy in zones 6 to 11, it needs little water once established;

Oklahoma redbud (*Cercis canadensis* var. *texensis* 'Oklahoma')—has compact growth (15' x 15'), dark wine red flowers, and good heat and drought tolerance in zones 6 to 9;

Western redbud (*Cercis occidentalis*)—a multitrunked 10' to 18' by 10' to 18' tree, hardy in zones 7 to 9, with bright magenta or rosy flowers, bluish green leaves, and reddish seedpods.

Potential problems: prune sparingly as they produce flowers only on the past year's growth.

DESERT WILLOW
Chilopsis linearis
Category: sun-loving tree
Use: for shade, on patio
Soil: any; moist and well-drained
Hardiness: zones 6 to 11
Mature size: 20' to 30' high by 20' to 30' wide

Desert willows offer a remarkable show of pink to rose-purple orchid-like flowers from late spring to fall. They are also treasured for their slender light green sickle-shaped leaves and twisted trunk. This remarkable plant, native to desert arroyos throughout the Southwest, can be trained as a single or multitrunked small tree. Shrub forms are also available. Desert willows are fast growing, often gaining 2' in height in a single year. The flowers are trumpet-shaped, 2" long, and bunched in clusters at branch ends; they attract a host of hummingbirds and butterflies.

Desert willows need plenty of sun and heat to thrive. Plant them singly or in masses, lined up along hot walls to soften glare, or as a screen, informal hedge, or tall border. Desert willows are also useful as wildlife habitat, for erosion control, and as windbreaks.

For best results, desert willows should be planted in spring after they have leafed out fully. Water frequently throughout the first spring. They require little maintenance, but their form can benefit from selective thinning for desired shape. Flowers produce long brown fluff-filled seedpods that persist through the winter. Some gardeners find these unattractive: remove them with a hand pruner. Horticultural varieties come in many colors from white to burgundy. To make sure you get your favorite flower color, choose plants in bloom. 'Lois Adams' is a podless variety with pale lavender and magenta flowers.

Potential problems: desert willows can develop root rot in poorly drained soils.

Desert willow (*Chilopsis linearis*)

ABOVE: Grapefruit (*Citrus* spp.)
BELOW: Crepe myrtle (*Laperstroemia indica*)

CITRUS
Citrus species
Category: sun-loving tree
Use: as patio tree or shrub, for edible fruit
Soil: well-drained
Hardiness: varies; zones 9 to 11
Mature size: varies

The best-known edible citrus fruits include oranges, grapefruits, limes, lemons, tangerines, mandarins, and tangelos; lesser knowns include kumquats, pomellos, citrons, and limequats. Imagine how much better they taste when you walk out the back door in your pajamas and eat them fresh off the tree! Wonderfully sweet citrus blossoms attract bees and other pollinators to the garden and perfume the air—there's nothing else like this fragrance in all the world. So if you are living in a climate where citrus thrives, count yourself lucky and enjoy the perks!

Citrus leaves are simple, shiny, bright green, and densely packed on smooth branches; flowers are creamy white in plentiful clusters. Fruits are ornamental in shades of red-orange, orange, yellow, and green, and come in all sizes (from tiny 1" kumquats to enormous 8" pomellos).

Plant citrus as hedges, screens, or as individual specimens. For small gardens, make the most of space with dwarf varieties planted in large containers or multiple-variety plants with several kinds of fruit grafted on one tree.

To flourish, citrus need full sun, good drainage, water, and fertilizer. Soils should always be kept moist with regular deep irrigation. Containers may need daily water. If your soils are slow-draining, plant on slopes, in raised beds, or in containers. For the best varieties, consult your local extension agent to find out which will work for you.

Potential problems: the lowest temperature most citrus plants will endure is 25 degrees; in colder locations, grow them in containers and move them indoors in winter or plant them in protected, walled courtyards and cover them on cold nights.

CREPE MYRTLE
Lagerstroemia indica
Category: sun-loving tree or shrub
Use: as patio tree or shrub, mass planting
Soil: any
Hardiness: zones 7 to 11
Mature size: 6' to 20' tall by 10' to 15' wide

Crepe myrtle has showy flowers, amazing bark, and glowing fall color. All summer, it is covered in long conical clusters of white, pink red, or burgundy flowers with crinkled, crepe-papery petals. Irregular patches of outer pale gray-brown bark fall away to reveal whimsical patterns of smooth buff to pink inner bark. In autumn, crepe myrtle's small oval leaves are bronze, then glossy green, and finally yellow, orange, or red.

Use crepe myrtles in full sun as flowering accents, patio shaders, and in mass plantings. In warm winter zones, they make beautiful street trees. Once established, they are drought tolerant. In cold winter areas, crepe myrtle stems die back to the ground, and the trees are treated as perennials. In the coldest winter areas (zones 4 to 6), flowering crabapples (*Malus* species) have the same landscape benefits as crepe myrtles—a huge floral display, beautiful bark, and good fall color. Crepe myrtle varieties include:

‘Acoma’—weeping branches, white flowers, dark red fall color (10' x 11');

‘Comanche’—deep coral flowers and orange-red fall color (12' x 13');

‘Petite’ series (‘Petite Embers’, ‘Petite Orchid’, ‘Petite Red Imp’, and ‘Petite Snow’)—shrubs with yellow fall color (5' tall x 4' wide);

‘Tonto’—large clusters of red flowers, red fall color (20' x 20');

‘Watermelon Red’—bright red flowers, yellow fall color, rounded tree form (25' x 25').

Potential problems: crepe myrtles prefer heat, well-drained soils, and regular moisture, but they tolerate clay soils. Give them regular, deep water to develop efficient root systems. Prune in spring to remove dead branches and improve form.

QUAKING ASPEN
Populus tremuloides
Category: sun-loving tree
Use: for mass planting, fall color
Soil: moist, well-drained
Hardiness: zones 1 to 8
Mature size: 20' to 60' tall by 15' to 20' wide

Aspens’ rounded leaves have flat stems that catch the wind and cause them to flutter, creating the most beautiful mixture of light and shadow you will ever see. These fast-growing trees are also loved for their golden yellow to orange fall color and stout powdery white trunks, punctuated with black eye-like markings.

Aspens are upright, deciduous trees with narrow crowns. The opening of their flowers in fuzzy catkins that spill down from bare stems heralds the arrival of spring. Soon, light yellow-green leaves sprout from shiny buds and quickly unfurl.

Aspens do best when planted in spring. Plant quaking aspen singly or in clumps; they spread by underground roots and will naturalize. Companion plantings can include red-twig dogwood (*Cornus stolonifera*), shrub cinquefoil (*Potentilla fruticosa*), western juniper (*Juniperus occidentalis*), lupine, fern-like meadow rue (*Thalictrum fendleri*), and hardy geranium.

Potential problems: they require regular water to establish themselves and need protection from several pests. In spring, look for tent caterpillars and oyster scale—tiny gray crawling insects that range from the base of the tree upward, eventually forming a scaly covering on the trunk. Young aspens are delectable fare for elk and deer—surround young trees with sturdy fencing. Sapsuckers damage bark and can kill young trees—protect trunks with tree wrap. Aspen trunks heal slowly; avoid injuring them.

Quaking aspen (*Populus tremuloides*)

VELVET MESQUITE
Prosopis velutina
Category: sun-loving tree
Use: mass planting or alone
Soil: does not tolerate poor drainage or heavy soils
Hardiness: zones 7 to 11
Mature size: 20' to 30' tall by 25' to 30'

Velvet mesquite is a fast-growing winter-deciduous native tree with a broad canopy that provides much-needed shade and a haven for birds and wildlife in desert gardens. It has feathery leaves and fragrant flowers in long creamy clusters that attract honeybees. Velvet mesquite is extremely drought tolerant; its roots may reach down 40' to access moisture. Thick dark brown bark forms long, narrow strips on old trees, providing distinctive character; trim branches up from the ground. Pruning to improve shape is best done in late summer.

Mesquites need full sun and good drainage. Best planting time is fall. After planting, water deeply every week for the first two years; shallow irrigation results in shallow roots, reduces ability to survive drought, and may lead to trees blowing down with high winds. In dry conditions, velvet mesquite is shrub-like. Regular water is essential to develop the tree form. Mesquite needs no fertilizer.

Shade beneath velvet mesquite is not dark—its canopy provides a protected growing space for succulents and perennials that might otherwise burn in the summer sun. Plant with agaves, cacti, aloes, and hearts and flowers (*Aptenia cordifolia*). The paired spines of velvet mesquite make it an excellent barrier plant.

Evergreen in mild-winter areas (zones 10 to 11) and faster growing than its native cousins, Chilean mesquite (*Prosopis chilensis*) lacks the distinctive bark. Honey mesquite (*Prosopis glandulosa*) is a medium-sized 30' high by 20' wide winter-deciduous tree, hardy in zones 6 to 11, with rounded form and wonderfully gnarled branches.

Potential problems: mesquites should not be planted near pools as their fuzzy flowers necessitate constant cleaning and clog filters.

PURPLE FLOWERING PLUM
Prunus cerasifera
Category: sun-loving tree or shrub
Use: for small spaces, color accent
Soil: any
Hardiness: zones 4 to 11
Mature size: 20' by 20'

Purple flowering plum is a small deciduous tree, covered with pale pink to white flowers in spring and deep purple leaves throughout summer. The bark is dark brown.

Purple plum needs well-drained soil and grows best with manure fertilizer. Plan for moderate growth; about 12" of additional height each year can be expected. Purple plum makes a lovely

ABOVE: Velvet mesquite (*Prosopis velutina*)
BELOW: Purple flowering plum (*Prunus cerasifera*)

lawn tree when planted in the midst of a drought-tolerant lawn of native blue grama (*Bouteloua gracilis*) or sheep fescue (*Festuca ovina*); be sure to leave a mulched zone free of grass around the trunk to prevent lawnmower injury. Green stems and sprouts may appear and should be removed to maintain purple color; to increase next year's bloom, prune just after flowering.

A background of purple plum's leaves will nicely set off bright green, golden, or gray-leafed shrubs and perennials. Many landscape cultivars are available. 'Atropurpurea' has a rounded habit and coppery leaves aging to dark purple, then turning red in autumn. 'Newport' has dark purple leaves and the greatest cold tolerance. 'Thundercloud' has a rounded habit, dark copper leaves, fragrant light pink flowers, and sometimes small red fruit. The darkest of all varieties, 'Krauter Vesuvius' has blackish-purple foliage and an upright, oval form with single light pink flowers.

Potential problems: should not be planted in a lawn that receives frequent irrigation.

'PURPLE ROBE' LOCUST
Robinia x *ambigua* 'Purple Robe'
Category: sun-loving deciduous
Use: in small areas
Soil: any; will grow in poor soils
Hardiness: all zones
Mature size: 40' by 30' wide

Purple Robe' locust is a drought-tolerant small tree with large 8" clusters of long-blooming fragrant showy purple flowers and large compound leaves that are reddish bronze in spring and yellow in the fall. This tree has an extensive root system that makes it useful for erosion control.

Trees require infrequent watering but grow faster with more water. In high-desert gardens, try 'Purple Robe' locust with a ground cover of silver-leafed prairie sagebrush (*Artemisia ludoviciana*) or yellow-flowered golden columbine (*Aquilegia chrysantha*). All locusts attract butterflies.

'Purple Robe' is a hybrid locust (*Robinia pseudoacacia* x *Robinia viscosa*). Other locusts for southwestern gardens include 'Decaisneana', with large pale pink flowers in 4" to 8" long clusters, and 'Idahoensis', with reddish-bronze new growth and bright magenta-rose flowers in 8" clusters.

New Mexico locust (*Robinia neomexicana*)—a deciduous 6' to 20' by 6' to 8' multistemmed native tree with long compound leaves and abundant spines; it bears 6" long clusters of pink to rose-purple flowers in the summer. It is hardy in zones 4 to 8 and makes an excellent background and barrier for shade to full sun in upland and mountain gardens.

Black locust (*Robinia pseudoacacia*)—a large, fast-growing 40' to 75' by 30' to 60' tree with white fragrant flowers. It can grow in the poorest soils and is adaptable to all zones; it takes conditions from desert heat to subalpine cold. The 50' tall by 25' wide 'Frisia' variety has red thorns and young leaves that emerge orange and mature to yellow and green.

Potential problems: none.

'Purple Robe' locust (*Robinia* x *ambigua* 'Purple Robe')

ABOVE: Coral vine (*Antigonon leptopus*)
BELOW: Virginia creeper (*Parthenocissus virginiana*)

VINES

✿

CORAL VINE
Antigonon leptopus
Category: sun-loving deciduous vine
Use: on trellis or arbor, as screen or accent
Soil: any; well-drained
Hardiness: zones 9 to 11
Mature size: 20' by 10' (but up to 40')

Coral vine is a winter-deciduous vine that grows quickly each spring to cover a fence, trellis, or ramada with bright green heart-shaped leaves. Throughout the summer, clusters of small, clear pink flowers trail down in 6"-long sprays. A native of Mexico, coral vine blooms bountifully during the hottest months of the year.

Coral vine can be planted as a flowering accent or trained over lattice or wire to provide summer shade for patios and outdoor living spaces, or used to screen utility areas and power poles. Like all climbing vines, coral vine can provide tall plant cover in small gardens where a shrub or tree of equal height would take up far too much space.

Plant coral vine in full sun in the hottest part of the garden in loose soil mixed with one-third its volume of composted organic matter; after watering in thoroughly at 4", add a layer of organic mulch to help keep soil cool and moist during the growing season. Apply composted manure or slow-release fertilizer only once a year in spring.

Coral vine 'Baja Red' has watermelon red flowers; 'Album' is a white-flowered variety. If you like the look of coral vine but have winter frosts, try silver lace vine (*Fallopia baldschuanica*), a 40' cold-hardy relative in zones 4 to 8 with similar growth characteristics and a summer covering of lacy cream-colored flowers.

Potential problems: needs support to climb; requires ample weekly watering during summer but can subsist on winter rains.

VIRGINIA CREEPER
Parthenocissus virginiana
Category: sun or shade vine
Use: as ground cover, climber, for fall color
Soil: any; moist or moderately dry
Hardiness: all zones
Mature size: to 40'

Virginia creeper's leaves, rather than flowers, are its main attraction. Each year, after its autumn display of vibrant scarlet, this extraordinarily fast-growing deciduous vine drops its leaves. In spring, broad compound leaves unfurl with bronze new growth, later maturing to shiny dark

Trumpet vine (*Campsis radicans*)

green. Flowers are greenish-gold and tiny, followed by clusters of dark blue circular fruits relished by birds. Hummingbirds and others build their nests in the shelter of this vine.

Virginia creeper needs regular water to grow, is not particular about soil, and will grow in full sun to shade. Virginia creeper can be a spreading ground cover or climbing vine. Its extensive roots make it an effective erosion control plant. It climbs with tendrils ending in suction discs and therefore does not require support. To minimize negative impacts on walls and wood, vines should be allowed to reach desired size, then pruned as necessary during the growing season to keep them within bounds, and cut back severely each winter.

Potential problems: in deserts, it needs protection from hot sun; give it a northern or eastern exposure.

TRUMPET VINE
Campsis radicans
Category: full sun to partial shade
Use: on trellis or arbor, as screen or accent
Soil: any; best well-drained
Hardiness: all zones
Mature size: 30'

Trumpet vine is a creeper with aerial rootlets that will attach to and climb wood, walls, or masonry. It is a sturdy plant whose deep red-orange trumpet-shaped flowers contrast beautifully with its shiny dark green leaves. The seedpods of trumpet vine are visually appealing as well. Hummingbirds are drawn to the 3" long flower tubes arranged in clusters at branch tips.

Trumpet vine is not particular about soil, but thrives in deep, open, fertile soils. In low deserts, amending soil with one-third its volume in organic matter, using organic mulches, and watering deeply will assure vigorous growth and bold bloom. Prune trumpet vine in spring to remove winter damage, renew growth, or control size and shape.

Potential problems: in hot desert areas, it is best to plant trumpet vine in cooler locations (try northern or eastern exposures) or partial shade.

Citrus trees need fertilizer, regular water, and a little special care, but will reward you handsomely (and deliciously!) for your efforts. White tree paint on the trunk of this orange tree prevents sunburn.

■ Troubleshooting in the Garden: Pests, Invaders, and Diseases

WEEDS

Check with your local master gardeners (see Resources section) to learn which noxious weeds are a problem in your area. A few plants that are quite attractive can be quite invasive in the garden. If you find a plant is taking over, remove it—it's probably not the best choice for you.

INSECTS AND DISEASES

Some things are actually easier in dry climates. Where water is limited and extremes of temperature are the norm, insects and diseases have a harder time getting a foothold. Many beginning gardeners panic at the sight of any insect in the garden. Most insects are just as busy as you are doing good work in the garden—they pollinate flowers so that fruit and seeds form, open up soil by digging in it, help to break down old plant materials into soil organic matter, and even make a meal out of other insect pests that might harm your garden. As a general rule, there are more beneficial insects in a garden than otherwise.

If you have any money left to spend once you've planted your garden, consider buying a binocular field microscope. Not only will it help you separate the good guys from the bad, it will give you insight into how insects work. Do they have a long tongue for nectar feeding, or chewing/piercing/sucking mouth parts? It will even allow you to see some of the smaller critters in action when you can't see what they're doing with your naked eye. You can also take insects (or good close-up digital photos) to your local nursery or agricultural extension office for identification.

THE GOOD GUYS

Beneficial insects and good garden health are the first line of defense against harmful insects and diseases. Next come low-impact garden practices like spraying and blasting with water and washing with household or insecticidal soap. Finally, a few commercially available substances—diatomaceous earth, horticultural oils, and neem oil and pyrethrins (both made of natural plant compounds, called botanicals)—can be used sparingly on insect pests if other means fail.

Natural insect repellents made at home by brewing a sun tea of the fresh or dried leaves of wormwood (*Artemisia absinthium*), tansy (*Tanacetum vulgare*), or painted daisy (*Chrysanthemum coccineum*) are also effective. Sprayed preventively, they don't kill insects. Instead they cause aphid colonies on roses and columbines to disperse. Compost teas, made by soaking finished compost in water, also benefit plant health and reduce insect and disease infestations. Apply these as a foliar spray with a small hand-sprayer or water them into each plant's root area.

Remember, you are a "beneficial" in your garden, and more than likely you are the most active one. Hand picking and washing are just two of the ways humans can reduce insects in a garden. As pointed out in the introduction, if pests do become a problem, most can be sprayed with soap, washed off with a blast of water, or wiped off with a wet cloth. One of the best means of control for larger insects is your hand—just pick them off of your plants. If you're too busy or too refined for this, try enlisting the help of neighborhood children. They're not at all squeamish and usually like such a challenge. A teacher I know achieved complete control of grasshoppers in her garden by paying the kids next door a nickel apiece for collecting grasshoppers.

Beneficial insects include assassin bugs (they kill the bad guys), ground beetles (they help break down garden debris into priceless soil organic matter), lacewings (don't be fooled by their fairy-like appearance and diaphanous green wings—they are killing machines), ladybugs (the immature ones look like spotted red and black alligators and are just as effective in scouring the area for dinner), parasitic wasps (these don't sting—but they do inject their eggs into other insects, which then hatch out and consume their hosts), hover flies, praying mantis, and walking sticks. Spiders are garden good guys, too—they eat many times their weight in insect pests. Planting "pollinator" plants to encourage beneficial insects also helps keep the balance in their favor. Birds, bats, and lizards eat many insects, so be sure to do all you can to encourage their presence in the garden.

As you spend time working outdoors, you'll be amazed at how many different types of bees there are. Most fruit trees and vegetables need pollination in order to set fruit—so you'll want to attract bees to your garden. Mesquite and brittlebush are two desert plants that bees love. Life can be hard for bees in the dry Southwest, so a shallow water source with some floaters (floating aquatic plants, flat pieces of balsa wood, or foam) will allow thirsty bees to drink without drowning. One warning: if you're clearing away brush to put in a new garden, be cautious. Notice where bees are landing: some ground-nesting bees will sting when provoked, particularly during hot times of the day. If any members of your household are allergic to bees, you'll want to exercise caution when selecting plants. Blue-flowering plants like rosemary, borage, salvia, and mint are surefire bee attractants; avoid planting these near paths or seating areas.

Healthy garden practices also reduce pests and diseases. Make sure plants are in the right place—particularly when it comes to their needs for light and shade. Avoid overwatering and heavy fertilizer use: both encourage luxury growth that is particularly vulnerable to insect attack and disease. Give plants proper spacing and good maintenance so that they are healthy and able to repel insects. Keep leaves free of dust. Like overwatering, drought stress makes all plants more susceptible to insects and disease. Be sure to provide just enough water to assure that plants are actively and healthily growing.

THE BAD GUYS

Most insects will come and go in the garden without your notice. Only a few are so common and destructive in the Southwest that they warrant mention here.

Aphids are small, soft-bodied insects with sucking mouth parts. They can be green, gray, brown, black, or even orange. All have two features in common: piercing mouth parts like the straws in juice boxes that let them drain the juices from your plants; and cornicles, twin tail pipes that are their identifying characteristic. Aphids are found on young flower buds, leaves,

PLANTS THAT ATTRACT BENEFICIAL INSECTS

Chances are you already have many beneficial insects in your garden area. You can help bring others in by including beneficial-attracting plants in your garden plans. Try to have several in bloom at all times during the growing season. The following plants are recommended by virtue of heavy use by many beneficials—bees, insects, bats, spiders, and birds:

- Agave, saguaro, and yucca—for nectar for bats
- mesquite (*Prosopis* species)—for bees, butterflies, and bird nests
- beargrass (*Nolina* species)—for bees and many other insects
- wild buckwheat (*Eriogonum* species)—for bees, butterflies, long-horn beetles, bee-flies, wasps, and birds
- Wood's rose (*Rosa woodsii*)—for native bumblebees and numerous other beneficials
- clover and alfalfa (*Trifolium* species and others)—for bees

- members of the parsley family (Queen Anne's lace, dill, anise, fennel)
- Rocky Mountain bee plant (*Cleome serrulata*)
- thistle (*Cirsium* species—try native species)
- tansy
- daisy-type flowers of all sizes, shapes, and colors (Cowpen daisy, feverfew, showy goldeneye, calendula, aster, coneflower, goldenrod, and yarrow, to name just a few)
- wild bee balm—(*Monarda fistulosa* and other *Monarda* species)
- sage and salvia
- pincushion flower (*Chaenactis* and *Scabiosa* species)
- desert bluebell (*Phacelia* species)
- verbena (*Verbena* species)
- mustard—sweet alyssum, mustards, radishes (allow the latter two to bolt and flower)
- borage—blue flowers attract bees

and shoots. They exude honeydew, which attracts ants and serves as the medium for black sooty mold. Washing away aphids, ants, and black sooty mold with common or insecticidal soap will usually do the trick. Soft new growth encourages aphids, so if you keep finding a lot of them, it's time to cut back on the fertilizer.

Tent caterpillars spin web tents on branch tips on such trees as Texas mountain laurel, pecan, aspen, and flowering crabapple. Look inside the webbing and you will see a lot of small caterpillars feeding on the wood. If you can reach the webs by hand or with a broom, pull them off the tree and dispose of them, caterpillars and all.

Heavy infestations of grasshoppers are one problem that can't be ignored. As with deer, elk, and gophers, look the other way for too long and your plants will be gone! Grasshoppers' effective chewing mouth parts inflict ragged-edged damage on leaves and frequently eliminate flowers. Broad-leaved, coarse-textured plants such as hollyhocks and mints are their particular favorites. Holes chewed around leaf edges are a sure sign grasshoppers have visited your garden, as is their large visible gray to black frass (grasshopper poop!). You may never even know you had grasshoppers if you manage to attract enough hungry birds—they'll do your dirty work for you without harmful chemicals and your leaves will remain unscathed. If birds aren't keeping up with the task, don't forget, recruit the neighborhood children! Nolo Bait or Semasphore (*Nosema locustae*, a biological control), can be effective applied at the right stages of grasshopper growth. It must be hand-broadcast when grasshoppers are young and reapplied as new grasshoppers hatch or move in. It is not harmful to wildlife or birds, but disrupts the eating processes of grasshoppers, causing them to weaken and die.

I know you don't want ants at your picnic. But before you bring out the arsenal of poisons frequently employed against them, consider the good things they do for your garden. Ants work the soil and add their bodies to soil organic matter, provide food for a host of beneficial creatures from toads to horned lizards, and actually plant seeds for you in the garden. Their seed-caching activities give the wildflowers just the conditions they need to germinate and grow. Yes, that's right: many native plant species depend on ants to cache seeds just below the soil surface—without them, many of the wildflower patches you've come to love would never grow and bloom. Ants are usually not a problem—although they may be harboring insects that are.

Ants are the cowboys of the insect world, and aphids, mealybugs, whiteflies, and some scale insects are the cattle. The ants protect their insect herds from rainfall and from your control efforts. In return they get a payoff—delicious, high-energy honeydew exuded by the insect pests. To prevent ants from maintaining herds of aphids, scale, or mealy bugs on your plants, blast pests and ants alike off with a powerful hose end spray. If the problem persists, try painting a circle of sticky barrier such as Tanglefoot around the bottom 3" of the woody portion of your tree or shrub. The ants get stuck and can't watch over their herd, and the other insects will just have to face up to life's perils on their own.

In all other cases, try to coexist with your ants. If you begin to dig a planting hole and find you've hit an ant colony (you'll know you have because they come streaming out, looking very agitated, trying to relocate their eggs), abandon planting. Just find a place at least a yard away where you can move the planting hole without disturbing the ants. If you plant too close to an anthill, they'll defend their territory by churning the soil continuously until whatever plant you've planted literally disappears below the soil surface. I know this from experience. This summer I've lost a coneflower, a soap plant, and a Virginia creeper in this very way!

One pest that is a problem in dry areas is spider mites. Mites are tiny eight-legged creatures smaller than the head of a pin. They look like tiny red spiders and leave very fine webbing in their wake. Damage to leaves is usually stippling—the appearance of little, light-colored dots on leaves and an overall bronzing of affected foliage. As a result of mite infestation, aloes develop contorted growth, agaves develop dead, corky pieces of tissue, and other plants exhibit stippled leaves and stunted growth. Spider mites thrive on dusty leaves. To prevent infestations, keep plants healthy and rinse dust from leaves regularly.

Tiny thrips are common on roses and citrus. You may not see them, but you will notice the stunted curling leaves and brown flower buds they cause. If you suspect thrips, shake the flower bud or leaf over a piece of paper. The tiny dark-colored spots that appear on the paper and begin to walk around are thrips. Thrips are drawn to blue traps placed near host plants in spring, before damage occurs. It's too late for trapping once they've worked their way into buds and leaf tissue. Prune away damaged parts and dispose of them away from the plant. Rake up fallen leaf and flower debris to prevent repeat infestation.

Scale insects sap a plant's strength by sucking its juices. They emerge as tiny crawlers in spring, then anchor permanently to plants with their sucking mouth parts and grow a protective cover that sheds water and may look either like a waxy shield (hard scale) or a soft cottony mass (soft scale). Oyster scale is a hard scale that attacks aspens, willows, currants, and goose-berries at mid to high elevations. Many succulents are infested by hard scale. Cottony cushion scale is a soft scale with an appearance similar to mealy bugs and giant whitefly. Cochineal is a soft scale found on prickly pears and chollas (*Opuntia* species). It is valued by some textile artists as a source of red dye. All scale insects are most vulnerable in their immature crawler stage. Crawlers can be blasted off with water or sprayed with horticultural oil, insecticidal soap, or botanicals. Hard scales can be scraped or scrubbed off woody stems with scrubber sponges or soap pads. On deciduous plants, they can be smothered with spray oils in winter.

Evergreen trees are subject to a variety of insect pests, particularly during drought. Borers are the larval stage of beetles and moths. They damage a variety of woody and succulent plants, including bulbs, cacti, yuccas, roses, ocotillos, aspens, and irises. Bark beetles can cause the death of ponderosa pine, piñon pine, and Arizona cypress trees. The best defense against bark beetles and borers is to maintain trees in good health with adequate moisture. Healthy trees can expel invaders and survive attack. In dry years, this means providing established trees with deep irrigation several times during the year to offset rain deficit. Save your money on pesticide injec-tions; they simply don't work. Once trees show symptoms of bark beetle infestation (exit holes, browning of needles) it is usually too late to save them. Be sure to remove any infested wood from the area or the beetles will spread to other trees. Western spruce budworm causes defoli-ation of spruce and Douglas fir and is common where the trees are grown with insufficient water or planted in overly hot locations.

Slugs and snails are not insects, but mollusks (like clams). Snails have shells and slugs do not. Both need moisture to live. They love to eat the tender, succulent parts of plants. By day, they hide; by night, they feed. The complete disappearance of young plants is evidence of snail and slug damage. In fact, you may think the seed you planted never germinated, as the snails and slugs mow down newly emerged seedlings while you sleep. Snails and slugs travel on a cushion of slime. Shiny trails on ground and leaves are evidence of their nighttime activities. Look also for holes in leaves and flowers. Snails love amaryllis, violet, and iris. Take a flashlight outside at night and you'll be rewarded with good picking, or leave out a saucer of beer near their favorite plants (they'll crawl in, drink, and die). A flat board propped up a couple of inches above the ground will encourage them to congregate during the wee hours; you can pick them off the bottom side when the sun shines. Birds, possums, raccoons, skunks, and other small mammals eat snails. If you have citrus trees, strips of copper attached around the base of trees will keep them from climbing up and damaging leaves.

Whiteflies are winged insects that resemble tiny white moths. When whitefly-infested plants are disturbed, the mature adults momentarily rise in a white cloud and then resettle. They thrive in mild winter areas, and thus frequent lantana, hibiscus, peppers, tomatoes, basil, lemon verbena, and other soft-leafed perennials. Check the undersides of leaves when you buy plants and reject candidates if eggs (they look like white circles with dark black centers) or nymphs are present. If you have whiteflies, soaps will eliminate immature crawlers, but adults are hard to control because they fly off at the slightest disturbance. Yellow sticky traps hung near infested plants successfully lure adults.

Giant whitefly is a relatively new southwestern pest. First found in southern California in 1992, it has made its way to parts of Arizona. The adult giant whitefly is large, up to $3/16''$ in size, and is slow to move around compared with other whiteflies. Nymphs (juvenile crawlers) produce long, hair-like filaments of wax up to 2" in length, which impart a bearded-looking covering to infested leaves. Giant whiteflies lay their eggs in spiral patterns on the undersides of leaves. This pest usually takes three to six months to become well established on a plant. Keep your eyes open—if you find giant whitefly in your garden, notify your local agricultural extension agents. Hose-end blasting and removal of infested leaves are as effective as any other means of control.

Scorpions live and multiply in the buildup of fronds of palm trees in hot areas. If your palm has persistent fronds, you'll want to schedule their removal regularly to keep scorpion populations from burgeoning in your garden. They don't harm plants, but if you've ever been sitting in a lawn chair by the pool with a cold drink in hand and had one of them tumble onto your lap or exposed flesh, you'll know you don't want them dropping in on your next garden party.

DISEASES

Plant diseases are the result of a harmful fungus, bacteria, or virus that only becomes a problem when it lands on the right host plant and finds favorable environmental conditions. Some plant diseases cannot be avoided. But most occur when a plant is either in a weakened condition, planted in a bad location, or given inadequate or inappropriate care. When plants are unhealthy, diseases stand a better chance of taking hold. Many diseases are caused by poor watering habits: too much water, too little water, water applied at the wrong time of day, or water that won't go away (poor drainage). Use of a soil moisture meter to check moisture levels can help you diagnose soil-water problems.

Water applied to the wrong part of plants can also lead to disease—powdery mildew, a white mold on leaves (common on crepe myrtles, coneflowers, roses, tall phlox, and bee balm) occurs when water sits on leaves, particularly in shady areas. Applying powdered sulfur on leaves and planting powdery mildew–resistant varieties can prevent this. Root rots can be bacterial or fungal and most frequently occur in heavy soils that retain too much water and not enough oxygen.

Discourage root rot pathogens by providing good drainage and just the right amount of water applied in cool morning hours. Aloe, cactus, paperflower, desert marigold, desert spoon, beard tongue, wild fuchsia, elm, Chinese pistachio, blue mist spiraea, and many native and drought-tolerant plants are quite susceptible to root rots. In fact, most land plants will eventually succumb to root rots if overwatered continuously or poorly drained. Crown and stem rots are similar to root rots. Planting at the right height and keeping mulches away from stems and crowns will prevent these.

PROTECTION AND WATER

Young plants in particular may need protection until they toughen up. Walls of water, shading, wind fences, floating row cover, and bark painted white can all help a plant establish itself in a tough environment. Apply mulch as soon as you plant and baby new transplants with frequent visits and frequent water. In dry climates, missing just one watering can mean death for new transplants.

Coarse sands drain quickly, but water has nowhere to go when there is an underlying caliche layer or hardpan. To test soil drainage, dig a hole 12" deep, fill it with water once. Let the water run through, then fill the hole again. If the hole has not drained after 24 hours, your soil has poor drainage. Consider planting in raised beds or on mounds where water will drain away.

If you notice your plants are growing poorly or have scorched-looking leaf tips and edges, look into your local water quality. Southwestern water can be alkaline (containing high concentrations of dissolved mineral salts) or saline. Some soils show white alkali salts brought to the surface by capillary action in winter. Salt buildup in soils depresses plant growth. If soils are reasonably well-drained and water is available, salts can be leached down below the rootzone by deep watering. Manure can be high in salts, too, so avoid using it as mulch or soil amendment where irrigation water or soils are salty.

Water high in sodium also limits plant growth and destroys soil structure. Unlike salt, sodium does not leach with water alone. A yearly application of gypsum or soil sulfur, followed by flood irrigation, removes sodium from the soil and improves soil structure and drainage. Gypsum is also effective in breaking down hardpan and caliche. Rainwater is salt free. If your irrigation water is highly saline or alkaline, collecting rainwater and using it for occasional deep irrigation is one way to reduce salt buildup in your soils. If leaching is not an option, salt-tolerant quail-bush and four-wing saltbush are large, fast-growing shrubs that tolerate salty soil.

PLANT NUTRIENT DEFICIENCIES

Only a few nutrient deficiencies are common in the Southwest, and these are easily treated. "Chlorosis" is the bleaching of green color from between leaf veins, and indicates iron deficiency. It occurs with rapid plant growth or when soil iron becomes less available with cold. Zinc deficiency results in stunting and leaf burn in pecan trees, and abnormally narrowed, pointed leaves with a mottled appearance at branch ends in lemon and lime trees. Because of simple chemistry, iron is tied up in alkaline soils. Soil sulfur (added as iron sulfate or chelated iron) acidifies soil and makes iron and zinc more readily available to plants. Yellowing of older leaves and slow growth point to a nitrogen deficiency. If this happens, fertilize. Symptoms of magnesium deficiency (common in roses in alkaline soils) are a yellow "V" within the margin of browned leaf tips. To treat or prevent this, water-in one-fourth cup Epsom salt (magnesium sulfate) for each plant.

■ Planting Southwest Style

As a general rule, the best time to plant is when plants will experience the least stress. Aim for a day when temperatures are not extreme, moisture is available, and humidity is reasonably high. Always plant during the coolest portion of the day at the most favorable time of year. Cacti need slightly different treatment. If placed in cold, damp soils they will rot. Planting during harsh summer conditions makes it difficult for them to become established. They need warm but not baking soils to stimulate growth. Plant them in spring or autumn in hot deserts and in summer in cold climates. Bare-root plants, including deciduous trees, are best planted in spring, before they leaf out.

When you bring plants home from the nursery, water them well and place them in a location with light shade or filtered light. You will find that they need frequent watering until planting. Most nurseries water several times a day to keep plants looking their best. It's much easier to keep plants adequately watered in the ground than in containers. Plant as soon as you can. Be sure to loosen soil to a depth of 6" to 12" with a garden fork before planting perennials, or deeper for woody plants. This will allow water and air into the soil. If your soil is heavy clay or fast-draining sand, work in one-third compost or composted manure to a depth of 12" as you loosen the soil; this will open up fine soils, allow sandy soils to hold more water, and provide a slow-release nutrient.

In the hot, dry Southwest, the way you handle plants while transplanting them is important. You can't get away with sloppy planting techniques here. Plants will die. Watch those roots! They can be cooked or killed with only minutes of exposure to hot sun or drying air, so don't leave containers lying on their sides in the sun when planting. To make sure you get water to the plants' roots, double-water containers just before planting (fill the container with water and let it run through, then fill again), and then double-water the planting hole. (If you have heavy soils, you will have to water the planting hole several hours before planting). When the time comes to take the plant out of the container and place it in the ground, do this quickly so root hairs are not exposed to drying air. Firm the plant in, then build a planting basin just a little bit larger in diameter than the rootball, and water-in thoroughly again immediately upon planting.

MAINTENANCE

Once the new plants have settled in, you can spend a lot less time working and a lot more time enjoying your garden. The more time you spend in your garden, the keener your observations will be and the better your plants will do. Getting to know your site and paying attention to what works and what doesn't are the best tools you have to help your garden age well. Good gardeners walk their garden regularly to see how plants are doing, hand-water or check irrigation systems when they are running, and fix little problems before they take hold.

I asked a county agricultural extension agent friend for his advice to beginning gardeners.

He gave a lot of good suggestions, but one jumped out at me. "If you can plant edible fruit trees, do so. There is no greater joy than picking your breakfast off the tree."

No matter what any gardening book says, maintain your garden to meet your own needs and it will give you many pleasures. If you enjoy seedheads or dried flowers, by all means leave them on. If you have fruit trees, it's best to contact your local agricultural extension and get the lowdown on timing of fertilizer application and pruning in local conditions. Apples, pears, peaches, cherries, and other deciduous trees are pruned during their winter dormant season. Citrus is best with minimal pruning; if you must remove a branch or reduce the size of a tree, prune in November. Deadheading, pruning, fertilizing, and mulching are all activities to fit into your schedule. Regular maintenance will keep your plants healthy and looking their best. But don't ever work so hard you find yourself avoiding going out into the garden. Now, promise me!

WHERE TO GET PLANTS

The Resources section lists some nurseries and catalog sources that come to you with my highest recommendation. I haven't visited everywhere, so rest assured there's plenty of room for you to discover your own favorites. Make it a habit to seek out new nurseries and talk to other gardeners about where they find plants. Botanical gardens and native plant societies schedule annual sales that are well worth the wait. Local garden clubs often have plants to share. Starting plants from seed and cuttings are both inexpensive ways to get plants. Check with your community college or agricultural extension to learn how.

Once you produce a surplus, try organizing your neighborhood for a garden-goods-and-plant swap. It's a great way to meet your neighbors and keeps items out of the landfill. People can take what they want, or nominal charges can be assigned, with proceeds going toward a good local cause like school playground equipment.

People are born to grow plants (we've been doing it for thousands of years). Gardens are made to be shared. Having a beautiful front yard; saving seeds; picking your own tomatoes fresh off the vine and whipping up a batch of salsa with backyard ingredients; sharing fruits and flowers with friends and neighbors; allocating garden resources to provide food, shelter, and habitat for local wildlife—all these activities in our gardening routine help grow community and bring the joy of a bountiful harvest into your home.

With some planning, some work, and a bit of patience, you'll have your first garden. By this time next year, you'll be entertaining, picking, cutting, eating, bird-watching, working, puttering, and relaxing in your own special space. Happy gardening!

Resources

NURSERIES

Shady Way Gardens
566 W. Superstition Blvd.
Apache Junction, AZ 85220
480-288-9655
One of the first growers of native plants in the
Phoenix area. Knowledgeable staff. Fun!

Baker's Nursery
3414 N. 40th St.
Phoenix, AZ 85018
602-955-4500
An old family nursery with a plant-loving staff,
great for all kinds of plants; good selection of
drought-tolerant and native plants.

Garden Territory Store
The Farm at South Mountain
6106 S. 32nd St.
Phoenix, AZ 85042
602-276-6360; www.thefarmatsouthmountain.com
Gardening shop, education center on organic
gardening, foods and herbs, all at a wonderful
historic farm and orchard.

Desert Survivors
1020 W. Starr Pass
Tucson, AZ 85713
520-884-8806; www.desertsurvivors.org
Wide array of native plants. This nonprofit also
employs the disabled and offers early childhood
development services to children and families.

Living Stones Nursery
& Plants for the Southwest
50 E. Blacklidge
Tucson, AZ 85705
520-628-8773; www.lithops.net/aboutus.htm
A great selection of native and adapted
drought-tolerant plants, along with a huge variety
of unusual succulents and "living stones."

Mesquite Valley Growers
8005 E. Speedway Blvd.
Tucson, AZ 85710
520-721-8728
Wide selection and knowledgeable staff.

Flagstaff Native Plant
and Seed
400 E. Butler Ave.
Flagstaff, AZ 86001
928-773-9406; www.nativeplantandseed.com
Native and adapted plants, many are locally
grown.

Warner's Nursery (Page and Flagstaff)
1101 E. Butler Ave.
Flagstaff, AZ 86001
928-774-1983
–and–
908 N. Navajo Dr.
Page, AZ 86040
928-645-3235
An extraordinarily good selection, beautiful
displays, and knowledgeable staff.

Chino Nursery (George Nakayama)
827 West Rd. 3 N.
Chino Valley, AZ 86323
928-636-2247
Specializing in shade and fruit trees.

Arizona Botanical
1601 Hwy. 89A
Clarkdale, AZ 86324
928-634-2166
Cactus and drought-tolerant plants only.
Interesting place!

Nursery Source, LLC
2945 Southwest Dr.
Sedona, AZ 86336
928-284-2600
General nursery with good selection of natives
and drought-tolerant plants.

Santa Fe Greenhouses
2904 Rufina St.
Santa Fe, NM 87507-2929
505-473-2700; www.santafegreenhouses.com
Great selection! Great staff! Mature xeriscape
demonstration garden.

Agua Fria Nursery
1409 Agua Fria St.
Sante Fe, NM 87501
505-983-4831
A great selection of native and adapted plants;
well-informed staff; excellent catalog.

Plants of the Southwest
(Santa Fe and Albuquerque)
3095 Agua Fria St.
Santa Fe, NM 87507
800-788-7333; www.plantsofthesouthwest.com
–and–
6680 4th St. N.W.
Albuquerque, NM 87107
505-344-8830
Experienced, with a great selection of
southwestern native, adapted, and edible plants
and seed.

Bernardo Beach Native Plant Farm
3729 Arno St. N.E.
Albuquerque, NM 87107
505-345-6248
Author Judith Phillips's nursery. Fantastic!

Dry Creek Garden Co.
7250 S. Virginia St.
Reno, NV 89511-1110
775-851-0353
A good selection of native plants, knowledgeable staff.

High Desert Gardens
2971 S. Hwy. 191
Moab, UT 84532
435-259-4531
High-desert natives and adapted plants.

Intermountain Cactus
1478 N. 750 E.
Kaysville, UT 84037
801-546-2006
Hardy cactus, yuccas, and agaves.

Edge of the Rockies Native Seeds
616 Ford Dr.
Durango, CO 81301
www.frontier.net/~lisa/
Native seeds from the Rocky Mountains to the Colorado Plateau.

MAIL-ORDER SUPPLIERS

High Country Gardens
800-925-9387
www.highcountrygardens.com
Luscious catalog of adapted and southwestern native plants. Incredible selection and info.

Native Seeds/SEARCH, Tucson, Arizona
www.nativeseeds.org/v2/default.php
Traditional southwestern heritage seeds.

Plants of the Southwest
www.plantsofthesouthwest.com
800-788-7333
Seeds of natives, ornamental wildflowers, and southwestern edibles.

Western Native Seed
P.O. Box 188
Coaldale, CO 81222
719-942-3935
www.westernnativeseed.com
Native wildflowers and grass seed; regional grass and wildflower seed mixes.

Rocky Mountain Rare Plants
1706 Deerpath Rd.
Franktown, CO 80116-9462
303-265-9263 fax
www.rmrp.com
Alpine seeds from around the world.

COOPERATIVE EXTENSION

This program, run through land-grant universities, assists local gardeners and farmers, and provides Master Gardener's training and plenty of scientifically based information and advice.

University of Arizona Cooperative Extension, http://cals.arizona.edu/extension; 520-621-7205

Colorado State University Cooperative Extension, www.ext.colostate.edu

University of Nevada Cooperative Extension, www.unce.unr.edu/; 775-784-7070

New Mexico State University Cooperative Extension, http://www.cahe.nmsu.edu/county/

Utah State University Cooperative Extension, http://extension.usu.edu/cooperative/; 435-797-1000

GARDENS

The Arboretum at Flagstaff, Flagstaff
4001 S. Woody Mountain Rd.
Flagstaff, AZ 86001-8775
www.thearb.org/; 928-774-1442
Annual plant sale first weekend in June; plant sales throughout summer.

Tohono Chul Park, Tucson, Arizona
602-742-6455, http://www.tohonochulpark.org
Demonstration gardens and nature trails; excellent sales nursery with hard-to-find desert plants.

Desert Botanical Garden
1201 N. Galvin Parkway
Phoenix, AZ 85008
www.dbg.org; 480-941-1225
Amazing collection of native and adapted plants exhibited on 50 acres.

Arizona-Sonora Desert Museum
2021 N. Kinney Rd.
Tucson, AZ 85743
www.desertmuseum.org; 520-883-2702
Natural habitat zoo, demonstration gardens, and hummingbird garden. More than 1,200 plant species.

Tuscon Botanical Gardens
2150 N. Alvernon Wy.
Tucson, AZ 85712
www.tucsonbotanical.org; 520-326-9686
Native and adapted plants. Cactus and succulent garden; xeriscape garden; compost demonstration; butterfly, wildflower and Mexican-American heritage gardens.

Denver Botanic Gardens
1005 York St.
Denver, CO 80206
www.botanicgardens.org; 720-865-3500
Inspirational design! Low-water use and demonstration gardens.

Wilbur D. May Center at Rancho San Rafael Regional Park
1595 N. Sierra
Reno, NV
www.maycenter.com; 775-785-5961
High-desert garden with average annual precipitation of 7″, located between the Sierra Nevadas and the Great Basin desert.

University of Nevada Las Vegas Arboretum
4505 S. Maryland Parkway
Las Vegas, NV 89154-0164
www.unlv.edu/facilities/landscape/arboretum.html;
702-895-3392
On-campus arboretum that spans 335 acres, and xeriscape demonstration garden.

Rio Grande Botanic Garden (Part of the Albuquerque Biological Park)
903 Tenth St. S.W.
Albuquerque, NM 87102
http://www.cabq.gov/biopark/garden/index.html;
505-764-6200
Native and adapted plants in a beautiful setting.

Red Butte Botanic Garden, University of Utah
300 Wakara Wy.
Salt Lake City, UT 84108
www.redbuttegarden.org; 801-581-4747
Native, drought-tolerant, and children's gardens. Wonderful mass plantings!

SUGGESTED READING

Brenzel, Kathleen Norris, *Sunset Western Garden Book* (Sunset Publishing Corporation, 2001).

Brickell, Christopher, and Judith D. Zuk, eds., *The American Horticultural Society A–Z Encyclopedia of Garden Plants* (Dorling Kindersley Publishing, 1997).

Busco, Janice K., and Nancy R. Morin, *Native Plants for High-Elevation Western Gardens* (Fulcrum Publishing, 2003).

Cromell, Cathy, ed., *Desert Landscaping for Beginners: Tips and Techniques for Success in an Arid Climate* (Arizona Master Gardener Press, 2001).

Irish, Mary, *Arizona Gardener's Guide* (Cool Springs Press, 2002).

Johnson, Eric A., and Scott Millard, *How to Grow the Wildflowers* (Ironwood Press, 1993).

Morrow, Baker H., *Best Plants for New Mexico Gardens and Landscapes* (University of New Mexico Press, 1995).

Phillips, Judith, *New Mexico Gardener's Guide* (Cool Springs Press, 1998).

Phillips, Judith, *Plants for Natural Gardens: Southwestern Native & Adaptive Trees, Shrubs, Wildflowers & Grasses* (Museum of New Mexico Press, 1995).

Index